THE
JEHOVAH'S WITNESSES'
NEW TESTAMENT

A Critical Analysis of the
New World Translation of the
Christian Greek Scriptures

SECOND EDITION

Robert H. Countess

Presbyterian and Reformed Publishing Co.
Phillipsburg, New Jersey

First printing, April 1982
Second Edition, January 1987

90   91   7   6   5

Printed in the United States of America

Library of Congress Cataloging-in-Publication Data

Countess, Robert H.
  The Jehovah's Witnesses' New Testament.

  Bibliography: p.
  Includes index.
  1. Bible.   N.T.   English—Versions—New World.
I. Title.
BS2095.N442C68   1986   225.5'2   86-25561
ISBN 0–87552–210–6 (pbk.)

CONTENTS

ABOUT THE AUTHOR

The author was born in Memphis, Tennessee, graduated from Huntsville High School (Alabama) in 1955, and served eleven years in the U.S. Army, most as a chaplain. Having begun formal higher education at Bob Jones University, he took the B.A., M.A., and Ph.D. in Religion—the last degree in New Testament Text. Later he took the Master of Liberal Studies degree from Georgetown University and the Doctor of Ministry degree from Drew University. Other graduate study includes University of Georgia, Westminster and Princeton Theological Seminaries, Vanderbilt University-Peabody College, and the University of Alabama in Huntsville.

He was Instructor in Greek and Chairman of the Foreign Language Department of Covenant College, Assistant Professor of Philosophy at Tennessee State University, Instructor in Greek at University of Tennessee at Nashville. Other teaching experience includes Northern Virginia Community College and the University of Alabama in Huntsville.

He was ordained into the Presbyterian Church in 1965, served churches in Tennessee, Virginia, and Alabama, and entered the Army chaplaincy in 1976, being assigned to duty in Virginia, Turkey, Germany, Kansas, and Alabama. In 1978 he affiliated with the Congregational Church.

Having traveled to some twenty-five foreign countries, he has also led tours to Greece, Turkey, and Israel. He recently participated in an archaeological dig in the Mt. Kosmaj region of Yugoslavia. Other scholarly activities include book reviews and articles to various journals and magazines and newspapers, visiting lecturer to several colleges and seminaries in the U.S., Germany, and Ireland. Presently, he is working to bring out a reprint of James Wilkinson Dale's five volume *magnum opus* on the Greek words associated with the term "baptize."

He is married to Patricia Davis Countess, and they have two sons, Timothy and Stephen.

Readers may correspond directly with Dr. Countess by writing P.O. Box 12451, Huntsville, Alabama 35802.

FOREWORD

It has been well said that a translator is a steward of another man's work and it is required in a steward that a man be found faithful. The average reader will readily grant that fidelity to the original and accuracy of rendering are essential requirements for any version of the New Testament. He will ask that the Scriptures be permitted to speak for themselves and that the translator not project himself unduly into his work. Above all, a translation of the Bible should not be made a sounding board for the erroneous views of the translator.

Readers who are familiar with faithful older versions should be prepared to recognize major doctrinal aberrations in newer translations; but not many readers today are adequately equiped to detect all the vagaries of translators and to test the claims that are made for the multitude of new versions which have been appearing since 1881. To assess justly and accurately the faithfulness of a modern version of the New Testament calls for scholarly competence and accomplishment in such studies as textual criticism and the grammar and vocabulary of New Testament Greek. In the case of the *New World Translation of the Christian Greek Scriptures,* readers untrained in such subjects will be aided immensely by the study which Dr. Countess has made. This well-organized, clear treatment of the Jehovah's Witnesses' version of the New Testament will give to laymen and scholars alike information indispensable for evaluating the claims that have been made for it.

John H. Skilton, Ph.D.
Editor, *The New Testament Student*

PREFACE TO THE SECOND EDITION

The present edition of *The Jehovah's Witnesses' New Testament* embodies all of the earlier text except for the correction of typographical errors noted by the author and readers. Special thanks go to Dr. Richard Taylor for many of these corrections.

On pages 6-7 I have presented my early effort at identifying the translators of the *New World Translation* and learning of their academic qualifications. I met with a stone wall consisting of adamant refusal and mortared with pious disclaimers about glory to God. In 1982 I learned the answers to my questions when I came to know Raymond Franz, formerly a member of the Governing Body of the Jehovah's Witnesses. He managed to resign and "retire" (as it were) and still take with him a large store of his file papers gained over a three-decade period.

For details of his experience and enlightenment I highly recommend his *Crisis of Conscience*.[1] On page 51 he asserts that his uncle Fred Franz "had been the principal translator of the Society's *New World Translation*. . . ." In footnote 15 he writes:

> *The New World Translation* bears no translator's name and is presented as the anonymous work of the "New World Translation Committee." Other members of that Committee were Nathan Knorr, Albert Schroeder and George Gangas; Fred Franz, however, was the only one with sufficient knowledge of the Bible languages to attempt translation of this kind. He had studied Greek for two years in the University of Cincinnati but was only self-taught in Hebrew.

As Ray and I have discussed this we both agreed that George Gangas' ethnic Greek background would have been of no necessary value for a translation of the Greek New Testament. I have discussed this matter with Witnesses who cannot understand the great gap between Modern Greek and that of the New Testament. I even offered to pay the tuition to study ancient Greek if one particular Witness would matriculate at a university in his city. He declined, preferring to compare different English versions instead.

This second edition is a pleasant surprise to both author and publisher, who alike had thought that a first printing would be a slow mover. Apparently, the work meets a significant need.

Opportunities to speak on radio, on television, in conferences, and at schools at home and abroad have been a great experience. Particular appreciation goes out to Martin Merriman and John May for organizing the first Dublin Conference on Cults and the Family. These Irish brethren have become warm compatriots.

Lastly, reviews have in general been positive, and I have found myself in agreement with some of the negative criticisms offered in a few reviews. We all learn when our perspective becomes improved.

Gratitude is in order to the publishers for their enormous effort in the correction process and that of publicizing this work to the reading public.

Robert H. Countess
8904 Seaton Drive, S.E.
Huntsville, Ala. 35802

PREFACE

The present publication deserves recommendation for two reasons and to two classes of people.

One reason is the desirability for all Bible readers to arrive at a reasonable evaluation of any and all modern translations of the Bible, of which there are at present a great number. One of them translates the original Scriptures very accurately in poor English. Another is a somewhat defective translation in excellent English. Others are irresponsible paraphrases. Some either sporadically or repeatedly mistranslate the text to make it support a theology not derivable from Scriptures. Every Bible reader ought to have some knowledge of these translations.

The second reason for commending this publication is that Dr. Countess gives a penetrating analysis of one version now used, if not by many evangelicals, at least by many people who study the Bible and who come to our doors to persuade us that Jesus Christ is not very God of very God. When they come (and where we formerly lived they came about once a month for a period of years), we should know ahead of time how they misinterpret John 1:1 and other verses which assert Christ's deity. Should we not be ashamed, if we know only one verse?

The two classes of people who can profit by this study are, first, seminary graduates who have had some instruction in Greek grammar. They know, at least, the difference between an article and a verb, and they may have met the adjective *anarthrous*. Thus they will know that the word *God* in John 1:1 does not suffer from "arthritis."

The second group of people who should read this material are the intelligent Christians who, without technical training, are nonetheless seriously interested in the accuracy of their English Bibles, and who therefore are patient enough to read something less slapdash than *The Three Musketeers*.

Indeed, these are the people whom I am most anxious to persuade. Even if Jehovah's Witnesses do not canvass your community, all Christians ought to know more about what the Bible teaches, particularly its doctrines of Christ and the Trinity. The present study does not by any means confine itself to John 1:1. Some of its questions are: Did the Divine Name, the tetragrammaton, occur in the Septuagint? Did Jesus ever pronounce that Name when he spoke in Aramaic? Did the unpronounced word occur in the original New Testament manuscripts? Jehovah's Witnesses answer, Yes, and in particular appeal to Matthew. They hold that our Greek texts have been tampered with.

But a Preface should not be a summary. One must read the book. And some, I am sure, will find it more rewarding than *The Three Musketeers*.

Gordon H. Clark, Ph.D.
Chairman, Philosophy Department
Covenant College

INTRODUCTION

Nearly fifteen years have elapsed since the content of this book was successfully defended for the degree of Doctor of Philosophy in New Testament Text.[1] During these years I have progressed toward a balanced and genial outlook on mission and culture. Progress—like medicine applied to a disease—can be painful even though the outcome is health. I feel good about my vocation and about the overall content of my dissertation research.

First suggestions for publishing the latter came from Gordon H. Clark and John Warwick Montgomery in 1966 after I delivered a paper to the Evangelical Theological Society.[2] That paper largely presented the content of chapter 4. At that time, however, the task of preparation for publication was far from my mind since I had undertaken a position at Covenant College teaching Greek and serving as chairman of the Foreign Language Department.

Dr. Clark's preface to this work is warmly appreciated. Likewise, I am grateful to John H. Skilton's writing the foreword because of his well-known expertise in text and translations. Dr. Skilton provided early encouragement to me toward academic pursuits, particularly when he asked that I serve as news editor of *The New Testament Student*. Appreciation also must be given to Bruce M. Metzger for helpful suggestions in the early days of 1964, when I cast about for dissertation topics. Recently, I met Dr. Metzger on the Princeton Seminary campus and we discussed a more careful wording of the title so that researchers might readily discover this book when researching Jehovah's Witnesses.

I thank Mr. Charles Craig for his enormous patience over several years while I sat on the galley proofs during several pressure-filled episodes in my life. Perhaps his patience stems from those days of Presbyterian and Reformed Publishing Company when he stored boxes of books alongside bags of potatoes at the grocery store next door. Whatever the case, he, his wife, and son Bryce have been most pleasant acquaintances for two decades.

---

1. Permission granted for publication by Bob Jones III, January 21, 1967. Dissertation was in partial fulfillment for the degree cited above at Bob Jones University, Greenville, South Carolina, awarded in June, 1966.

2. "The Translation of ΘΕΟΣ in the *New World Translation*," *Bulletin of the Evangelical Theological Society* X, 3 (Summer, 1967):153-60.

The original dedication was to my wife Pat, for she—like so many others' wives—put me through graduate school. Eventually I got even and put her through library science school so that she could do the index. For her support over the years I dedicate this volume to her.

This book goes forth with both eagerness and trepidation. Eagerness is present because of those who have encouraged publication and because of a perceived need for this kind of technical treatment of the *New World Translation*.[3] But there is trepidation because of the length of time that has elapsed since the original research and writing. Doubtlessly, most everyone who rereads his or her dissertation so many years later will have misgivings about some of the style, content, and conclusions and, if given the opportunity, would make many changes. These too are my thoughts and they grow out of what may very well be normal intellectual an theological development over two decades rather than an insecurity about the quality of the work itself.

Having said the foregoing, I reaffirm the general style, content, and conclusions of the original work, which was entitled *The New World Translation: A Critical Analysis*. Careful readers will want to examine the content and to test my conclusions about this version of the New Testament. Jehovah's Witnesses and their green colored Bibles are present in nearly every community, and a phone request to a Kingdom Hall will enable a reader to secure the loan or purchase of a copy. The edition I used as the basis for my research is that of May 1, 1951, containing a very important 21-page appendix (unfortunately omitted in later editions).

Now a word about the many editions and revisions by the Watchtower Bible and Tract Society. First, *most changes are not major*. Jesus is still "a god" in John 1:1, for example. And if a Witness asserts that revision continually takes place because of new data and insights, then obviously the question arises which arises in every *authoritarian* institution: Will future changes negate or contradict what is presently espoused? Since the Society is both authoritarian and dogmatic, the "witness-ee" ought always raise this question. For why cannot new data and future insight lead Society translators to the revision: "and the Word was God"? Clearly, one of the

---

3. I wish to acknowledge my appreciation to the Watchtower Bible and Tract Society for giving permission to quote from this publication in a letter dated November 12, 1980.

conclusions of my research is that the Society translators lacked crucial insights into Greek grammar at places.

Second, I am not aware that the Society has revised its basic principles regarding text interpolation, the Divine Name, and bias against traditional terminology. For example, they still refuse to employ the word "church" in a good sense.

In conclusion to the above, whatever edition of *NWT* that the reader confronts, my advice is to ignore peripheral revisions and get to the core translation, such as "a god" and the *NWT*'s 94 percent unfaithfulness to its own stated principle concerning the anarthrous θεός. If one does this, then the datedness of my work should not present a large problem.

Perhaps a brief word is appropriate at this point about the divine name. Chapter 3 treats of *NWT*'s so-called "restoration" of the divine name Jehovah to the New Testament. As for vocalization of the tetragrammaton, I relied upon a very old work by Gustaf Oehler (1883) whose position, I still judge, is adequate for my purposes, since I am not primarily concerned, as the Jehovah's Witnesses are, with *how* JHWH might have been pronounced. For readers who are so inclined, I recommend a recent article by Barry Beitzel in the *Trinity Journal* (vol. I, no. 1, pp. 5-20) entitled, "Exodus 3:14 and the Divine Name: A Case of Biblical Paranomasia."

One also might find value in consulting Jacob Milgrom's "The Temple Scroll" in *Biblical Archaeologist* (vol. XL, no. 3, pp. 105-20), in which he briefly comments on the form of the tetragrammaton in canonical and non-canonical Dead Sea Scroll literature; and also George Howard's "The Name of God in the New Testament," in *Biblical Archaeology Review* (vol. IV, no. 1 [March 1978], pp. 12f.). He concludes that only a discovery of a New Testament manuscript with the Hebrew lettering for Jehovah will enable us to know with certainty about this debate.

When last in Jerusalem (1979) I reexamined the Dead Sea Scroll fragment 4 Q LXX Lev.[a] on display at the Shrine of the Book museum. According to *NWT* theory, one would expect to find JHWH in Hebrew letters amidst the surrounding Greek Septuagint text. There is no Hebrew lettering. With the Essean commitment to strictness in religious matters, it seems reasonable that they would have inserted the Hebrew form of the tetragrammaton rather than using the Greek alphabet uniformly. For my part, however, I do not want to infer overly much from this manuscript about the autographa of the

Septuagint—which are, to our knowledge, no longer extant. Already, I believe that the *NWT* translators have inferred from Papyrus Fouad 266 that which supports their prejudice: to wit, that the presence of the Hebraically written tetragrammaton in *a* manuscript fragment justifies the assumption that the original manuscripts were written in the same manner. A fragment or fragments do not a corpus make.

For my purposes, vocalization itself is irrelevant to both text and theology. What *is* relevant is whether or not *NWT* translators can justify their 241 *interpolations* of "Jehovah" (and "Jah") into an English translation of the New Testament *when it is obviously done on the basis of religious preference and not textual evidence*. What would happen if Calvinists or Arminians or other interest groups were to interpolate their theological special terminology into a New Testament translation and then seek to justify such on the basis of sixteenth- to nineteenth-century written systematic theologies? The outcry of condemnation would be an uproar—and properly so.

I solicit from readers *their* insights, data, and counter-arguments on the major positions taken herein, because I regard highly the reasoned disagreements that come from the community of scholars. Such matters may be communicated directly. In this regard I further wish to authorize reproduction by photocopying of any or all of the contents of this work. I ask only that accurate source citation be given to both author and publisher.

The bulk of the material in this work will profit, most of all, those who have some facility with New Testament Greek. Clear, logical reasoning will be required in order to follow out certain arguments. For those without any understanding of Greek, earnest effort may lead to great profit, particularly in chapters 4, 5, and 6.

Lastly, this work goes forth with the prayer that seriously thinking people will be challenged radically to examine the grandiose claims of the Watchtower Society for its New Testament; and that upon such examination, everyone will conclude that of all the praiseworthy English translations available for study, preaching, and teaching, THE *NWT* IS NOT ONE OF THEM. *NWT* is, in some ways, like milk, but milk with an admixture of arsenic. Milk by itself can be wholesome, but this kind of mixing could very well prove injurious to one's health.

Chapter 1

THE PROBLEM AND DEFINITION OF TERMS USED

English translations of the whole or almost all of the New Testament since 1881 have numbered one or more per year. Although a few of these translations are the products of Roman Catholic scholars, the majority are the work of scholars within the Protestant denominations. In 1950, there appeared the *New World Translation of the Christian Greek Scriptures*,[1] a product of the Jehovah's Witnesses. This group can lay claim to being the first of the cults[2] to produce *in toto* its own translation of the New Testament.

I. *The Problem*

Statement of the problem. The essence of the claims of NWT—that it is an honest, reasonable, consistent, modern, unbiased, scholarly translation of the New Testament—precipitates the problem encountered in this thesis. That these claims are admirable no one will controvert; however, if this translation *is* all of these, then it is undoubtedly the first ever to meet such standards. Such claims are good, if verifiable, and, in order to verify them, one must investigate them.

Specific considerations which formed a basis for an answer to the general problem are: (1) an examination of textual principles and text; (2) the insertion of the Divine Name "Jehovah" where the Greek text reads κύριος or θεός; (3) an *a priori* anti-trinitarian view that manifests itself in the translation; (4) an anti-church or anti-tradition avoidance of accepted terminology in spite of an avowal of literal translation.

Need for this study. Were it a fact that the Jehovah's Witnesses phenomenon is but an insignificant cult largely confined to a small area in the United States or some other part of the world, there should be little cause for a critical study of this nature. However, the contrary is manifestly the case. The Witnesses are not insignificant. They constitute a cult, although their

---

1. Hereinafter this translation will be designated NWT.
2. A "cult" is defined as a dissenting party from an established church and espousing manifestly unorthodox doctrines. A better term, in my opinion, is "distinctive faith group," since this avoids a value-laden, and often self-serving, label.

name is often a byword, which has made its presence felt in nearly every community in the United States and in most countries without and within the Iron Curtain. Perhaps it should be noted that their insignificance has in part led to their significance. Confessedly, the Witnesses recruit more adherents from the so-called "churched" than the wholly unchurched. The more the Witnesses are regarded insignificant, the more insidious will be their significance, as they successfully prey upon uninstructed church attenders.

On the basis, then, of their claim to have such a faithful translation, their frequent and scholarly sounding allusions to Greek while proselyting, and their phenomenal growth, the Witnesses with NWT in hand present to many a highly impressive and effective witness for their position, and therefore called forth a study of this nature.

Previous studies. While there exists no overwhelming accumulation of works on the Jehovah's Witnesses, neither is there a dearth of them. However, the majority of books and articles this investigator consulted deal with doctrine and not with the NWT. Of the works that have taken NWT into account, only four may claim any right to be mentioned here. Taking them in the order of their publication, they are Walter R. Martin and Norman H. Klann's *Jehovah of the Watchtower;* Bruce M. Metzger's article, "The Jehovah's Witnesses and Jesus Christ," in *Theology Today;* Walter E. Stuermann's *The Jehovah's Witnesses and the Bible;* and Anthony Hoekema's *The Four Major Cults.*

Martin and Klann teamed up to produce a highly useful and devastating work for the pastor or layman to use in combatting the Witness phenomenon. Most of the book traces Witness history, and presents and refutes their doctrines. There is a thorough presentation of the John 1:1 translation of NWT with a good discussion of grammatical points. However, this chapter is presented only in so far as it is tangent to the overall doctrinal purpose of the entire book.

Metzger, opposing the Jehovah's Witness basic error, which he considers to be the Person of Christ, presents his case in twenty pages of *Theology Today.* However, only seven pages properly deal with NWT. This small section too concerns John 1:1, and in it one finds Metzger availing himself principally of Colwell's rule.[3]

---

3. See chapter 4 of the thesis.

Stuermann wrote two articles for *Interpretation,* but published together in a thirty-one-page monograph they bear the title, *The Jehovah's Witnesses and the Bible*. Probably half of this work treats of doctrine and the NWT Old Testament, thus leaving the remainder for the New Testament. He discusses briefly the Foreword, textual principles of translation, symbols, and the apparatus, always candidly citing the merits and demerits of NWT.

Anthony Hoekema has produced what should prove to be the most valuable work of its kind. In approximately 150 pages devoted to Jehovah's Witnesses, Hoekema provides an exhaustive study of Jehovah'sWitness primary source material. Moreover, he writes lucidly, in a scholarly fashion, and from a Reformed point of view. Furthermore, and in keeping with his purpose, he gives the reader a work that is much like that of Martin and Klann: doctrinal. Therefore, one does not expect to find a thoroughgoing analysis of NWT. Where Hoekema does review NWT, he makes use of Colwell and Metzger, who wrote before him. The great value seen in his treatment of NWT is that he demonstrates irrefutably the superimposed doctrinal bias of the Witnesses upon their translation.

Delimitations. The volume chosen as the basis of this study is the *New World Translation of the Christian Greek Scriptures* published in 1950 and revised May 1, 1951, and not the *New World Translation of the Holy Scriptures* published in 1961, which includes a revision of the former plus the Old Testament, and since the 1961 edition is only a peripheral revision of the former edition, the 1951 volume has been selected. Moreover, this edition contains a Foreword with a detailed discussion of the Divine Name, as well as a most interesting Appendix.

In the 1961 Bible the Foreword and most of the passages discussed in the Appendix of the former edition have been excluded. That the translators have not basically changed the work is plain to see, for the latest edition does not retract the Foreword or Appendix of the earlier, nor has the translation been essentially altered.

Until 1950 the Witnesses used the King James Version and the American Standard Version of the Bible, the latter with their own footnotes added. As stated above, the first edition of NWT appeared in 1950. Within a year it was revised, but only negligibly.[4]

---

4. The only noteworthy change appears on p. 768. In the first edition there was under Matt. 10:38 a discussion concerning the *crux ansata* with accompanying illustration.

The present study must of necessity limit itself to certain aspects of NWT. Clearly out of the question is an exhaustive investigation and presentation of every chapter, verse, and type of construction in NWT; however, the investigator is hopeful that he has presented enough aspects of NWT so that a valid, objective judgment may be made of the entire work.

Method of procedure. The method of procedure which has been followed in this thesis is this: First, there is a discussion of the text and principles of textual criticism adopted by NWT. Included also in this chapter is a discussion of the aim of the translators, their identities, the style of the translation, opinion of other translations, additions to Scripture, inconsistencies in translation, and the matter of chapters, versification, and orthography. Investigation has attempted to determine if NWT has sometimes avoided the basic canons of textual criticism or misapplied them, especially with regard to the citation of manuscript witnesses.

Second, it has been necessary to present much of the Foreword of NWT and discuss the Appendix on Matthew 1:20 in order to place in perspective the presence of the Divine Name in NWT. Although a matter of chapter three, it was deemed necessary to present and judge NWT's citation of certain medieval Hebrew translations of the New Testament as valid testimony. Also, germane to this chapter was the Divine Name—if it came— from the lips of Jesus. The real issue of this section has been seen to be a theological one and not a textual one. The writer has endeavored to demonstrate that at the base of the "restoration" of the Divine Name to the text of the New Testament lies a rationalistic, *a priori* unitarianism.

Third, the Appendix to John 1:1 has been presented, because the theology and reasoning behind the translation provided much proof showing the biased character of NWT. The method adopted to point up how consistent NWT has been regarding this Appendix was to note each of the 1,303 occurrences of θεός in the New Testament whether arthrous or anarthrous, and the NWT rendering of it in view of the principle enunciated in the John 1:1 Appendix. Furthermore, it was necessary to discuss the Greek article, especially its syntax as it is tangent to the construction of John 1:1.

Fourth, there have been set forth examples to show whether or not the doctrine of the deity of Christ and the Holy Spirit has suffered or been excised by NWT translators. In connection with this point the investigator endeavored to establish exegetically this doctrine of deity as it relates to the

Son and the Holy Spirit.

Fifth, there has been a presentation of examples of paraphrase in NWT where a much more literal rendering is possible. In this connection there has been noted an aim of the Foreword regarding the paraphrase; and also noted that there is present an attitude of anti-traditionalism regarding generally accepted terminology.

II. *Definition*

New World. The basis for this part of the title is evidently II Peter 3:13, which is quoted in full on the title page: "BUT THERE ARE NEW HEAVENS AND A NEW EARTH THAT ARE AWAITING ACCORDING TO HIS PROMISE, AND IN THESE RIGHTEOUSNESS IS TO DWELL." New World must refer, then, to the final, heavenly state.

Translation. This word may bear its normal meaning, as it is abundantly evident that the translators have made use of the Greek New Testament and have endeavored to bring out various nuances of the Greek language.

The Christian Greek Scriptures. The Foreword of NWT defines succinctly the meaning of this phrase: "Called 'Christian' to distinguish them from the pre-Christian Greek Septuagint translation of the inspired Hebrew Scripture."[5]

A Critical Analysis. The NWT will be criticized, or judged, carefully, primarily on the basis of the Greek text, and consequently analyzed, or separated, into sections dealing with specific problems.

---

5. *New World Translation*, p. 5.

Chapter 2

TEXT AND PRINCIPLES OF TEXTUAL CRITICISM

A prerequisite to a translation of the New Testament is the settlement upon a particular edition of the Greek text and upon certain textual principles. This chapter will concern itself with the Greek text adopted by NWT and the canons of textual criticism, whether they be explicit, implicit, or inferential. Primarily, the Foreword of NWT will provide the source material necessary to this chapter. The Appendix and certain footnotes to the text also will furnish relevant material. The three main inquiries will concern (1) the translators—their identity, their aims, and their opinion of other translations; (2) the text—the basic text, the use of Hebrew translations, the physical layout of the translation, and its praiseworthy features; and (3) textual principles.

I. *The Translators*

Every translation of the New Testament is either a complete translation from the original language or a revision of a former translation or revision; and it is the work either of a single translator or of a group of translators. A translation is, furthermore, either a private undertaking or the work of a foundation, or a denominational project.

Identity

The NWT resembles most nearly the work of a denomination. No private individual has translated it; NWT is the fruit of the New World Bible Translation Committee.[1] What most other translations or editions have been wont to do, NWT has chosen *not* to do—there is no listing or acknowledgment of the translators. Since the Foreword does not disclose why this is so, this investigator asked the Watchtower Bible and Tract Society of New York for the identity and academic qualifications of the NWT translators. The following paragraph is excerpted from the Society's reply:

---

1. *New World Translation*, p. 6.

The *New World Translation of the Holy Scriptures* is issued to glorify or memorialize the names of no men. Therefore, the men who compose the translation committee have indicated their desire to the Society's Boards of Directors to remain anonymous and specifically do not want their names to be published while they are in life or after death. The purpose of the translation is to exalt the name of the living true God and spread the knowledge of his kingdom by Jesus Christ. This translation, although it does not headline any highly respected names as translators, will still commend itself to every honest searcher for its faithfulness, courage and correctness. In the several volumes of its original edition it is buttressed with copious cross references and explanatory notes to show the reasons for its various renderings. Further, the Watchtower Society in publishing this translation backs up the translation and is ready to give answer to any questioner regarding the translation's accuracy—1 Pet. 3:15.[2]

As one would expect from reading this paragraph, the translators' identity has been kept not only from the public, but also from the rank and file Witness constituents. One can almost say with regard to this matter what Origen remarked concerning *Auctor ad Hebraeos,* "Only God Knows."

Opinion of Other Translations

The translators of NWT are aware not only of the existence of numerous English translations but also of the keenness of rivalry among them. Nor are they blind to the fact that "all these have had their own commendable features." These translations, it is said, have largely met the needs of their day and they have accomplished and yet will accomplish much good.[3] To some degree this tribute is incumbent upon the Witness translators. For two reasons, at least, is this true: (1) Were they not to acknowledge the value of preceding translations, they would be begging the question—Did not anyone have God's Word in translation form for the nineteen and one-half centuries preceding the advent of NWT? And (2) for half a century the Witnesses used two of these translations—the King James Version and the American Standard Version.

This praise, however, is not without qualification, for from the same paragraph come these words:

---

2. Watchtower Bible and Tract Society (personal letter, unsigned; Brooklyn, N. Y., Sept. 27, 1963).

3. *New World Translation*, p. 5.

But honesty compels us to remark that, while each of them has its points of merit, they have fallen victim to the power of human traditionalism in varying degrees. Consequently, religious traditions, hoary with age, have been taken for granted and gone unchallenged and uninvestigated. These have been interwoven into the translations to color the thought. In support of a preferred religious view, an inconsistency and unreasonableness have been insinuated into the teachings of the inspired writings.[4]

Having read this statement of the problem, one receives the impression that "a greater than Solomon is here." Despite the value which inhered in these works, NWT says, they were inextricably weighed down with a "preferred religious view."

Aims

The translators have clearly stated their aims for this translation in the Foreword. Numbering six, these aims are generally laudable. The first aim is to avoid the "snare of religious traditionalism" which has permeated every preceding translation.[5] NWT, according to the translators, is one work that will demonstrate its freedom from all religious bias and foregone conclusions.

A second aim is that of modernity. In view of the progress of a living language, with its changes in the meanings of words and idioms, a new and up-to-date rendering of the Scriptures is needed to make them fully alive and interesting to the understanding.[6]

Third, NWT aims at consistency:

Our primary desire has been to seek, not the approval of men, but that of God, by rendering the truth of this inspired Word as purely and as consistently as our consecrated powers make possible. There is no benefit in self-deception. More than that, those who provide a translation for the spiritual instruction of others come under a special responsibility as teachers before the divine Judge. Hence our appreciation of the need of carefulness.[7]

Tangent to this aim is that of assigning to each major Greek word one

---

4. Ibid., p. 6.
5. Ibid.
6. Ibid., p. 5.
7. Ibid., p. 7.

meaning and consistently maintaining this one meaning in the translation as far as the context allows.[8]

Fifth, NWT has attempted not a mere paraphrase but as literal a translation as possible. "As literal as possible" is explained to mean "where the modern English idiom allows and where a literal rendition does not for any clumsiness hide the thought."[9]

Finally, the translators have declared themselves to be against "taking liberties with texts for the mere sake of brevity or short cuts and against substitution of a modern parallel, where the rendering of the original idea makes good sense."[10]

II. *The Text*

Basic Text of Westcott and Hort

Because of its confessed excellence, the Greek text that was used as the basis of the New World Translation was the "widely accepted" Westcott and Hort text (1881).[11] In a footnote acknowledgment is made to the uncompleted work of S. C. E. Legg, which is simply the text of Westcott and Hort with Legg's own thesaurus of variant readings in the *apparatus criticus*. To date, only Matthew and Mark have been completed.[12]

Other editions of the Greek Testament taken into consideration include the eighteenth edition, 1948, of D. Eberhard Nestle's *Novum Testamentum Graece,* the Spanish Jesuit Jose Maria Bover's *Novi Testamenti Biblia Graeca et Latina,* 1943, and the 1948 printing of the sixth edition of *Novum Testamentum Graece et Latine* by Jesuit Augustinus Merk.[13]

The Westcott and Hort text has not been slavishly followed: "Where we have varied from the reading of the Westcott and Hort text, our footnotes show the basis of our preferred reading."[14] Especially is this true with regard to rendering the Divine Name, for on over two hundred occasions the

---

8. Ibid., p. 9.
9. Ibid.
10. Ibid.
11. Ibid., p. 8.
12. Ibid.
13. Ibid.
14. Ibid.

basic Greek text is rejected in favor of the readings found in certain Hebrew translations of the New Testament.

Hebrew Translations

The use of Hebrew translations of the New Testament by NWT translators was mentioned above. For the moment these will only be noted and briefly described. Table I on page 101 lists these translations by name, date, and the symbol assigned to each by NWT. Details concerning the reason for adopting these translations at times must wait until chapter 3, where full discussion of the Divine Name will be made. The translations are designated with the symbol "J" because it corresponds with the initial letter of the tetragrammaton.[15] The majority of these translations were either the sole work of Jews and Jewish Bible societies or works completed by a Christian translator after having been begun by Jews. One may conclude that as a whole these works were for the benefit of Hebrew-speaking Jewish people.

Versification, Chapter, Proper Names

The NWT follows the chapter and verse numbering of the King James Version in order to make for easy comparison between the two. However, unlike the latter, the NWT follows the paragraph method and not the method that makes each verse a separate paragraph in itself. Paragraphing has been preferred "for the proper development of a complete thought in all its context." Concerning proper names, NWT has chosen to follow mainly the Hebrew spelling rather than the Greek, which imitates the Septuagint.[16]

Merit

The expressed aims of the translators of the NWT are highly laudable; the extent to which those aims were realized will be examined in the chapters that follow. One virtue of the NWT, however, may be mentioned now. Insofar as the translators

> . . . have avoided the rendering of two or more Greek words by the same English word, for this hides the distinction in shade of meaning between the several words thus rendered, . . .[17]

---

15. Ibid., p. 21
16. Ibid., p. 10.
17. Ibid., p. 9.

they must be praised. This approach indicates commendable interest in the English reader who has no orientation in the Greek New Testament. The translators also point out in the Foreword that "attention has been given to the tenses of verbs to bring out the intended description of the action, position or state."[18]

The NWT must be commended also for attempting to overcome in its *apparatus criticus* a most frustrating practice found in many English versions. That practice is the use of the phrase, "Other ancient authorities read. . . ." The practice of NWT is to cite manuscripts and versions by their proper designations.

The NWT translators share unashamedly their common commitment—with many evangelicals—to the inspiration and inerrancy of the Bible. On the first four pages of the Foreword, "inspired" or a cognate of it appears more than ten times. Regarding the New Testament the Foreword says:

> The original writings of the Christian Greek Scriptures, commonly called "The New Testament," were inspired. No translation of these sacred writings into another language except by the original writers, is inspired.[19]

A footnote on the same page asserts inspiration for the Old Testament as well: "Called 'Christian' to distinguish them from pre-Christian Greek Septuagint translation of the inspired Hebrew Scriptures."[20]

Finally, the NWT translators showed themselves courageous in omitting certain poorly attested verses traditionally accepted because of their presence in *Textus Receptus*. Most outstanding are Matthew 6:13b; Mark 16:9ff.; John 8:1-11; Acts 8:37; 9:6a; 15:34; and I John 5:7b, 8a.[21]

III. *Textual Principles*

It is not possible to engage in serious Bible translation and at the same time disregard the discipline of textual criticism. For, contrary to the opinion of many, this discipline is characterized not by negative considerations but by positive considerations. Its aim is not to destroy the Scriptures, but to

---

18. Ibid., p. l0.

19. Ibid., p. 5.

20. Ibid.

21. On page 786 of NWT there is an appendix explaining the evidence against the I John 5:7-8 passage.

restore, insofar as possible, the *ipsissima verba* of the autographa. This discipline desires to go back beyond the text-type of the Middle Ages and beyond that of the fourth-century uncials; it desires to reach the text of the first Christian century, the era which gave birth to the New Testament.

In order to reach this goal the translator must face the tremendous mountain of New Testament manuscripts—some 13,000, containing all or part of the New Testament. Since no single translator or group of translators can make use of all these at one time, all translators must to some extent accept the consensus and product of textual scholars who have preceded them. To vary a translation at any one point from the chosen edition of the Greek Testament is to imply a reason for doing so—a reason based on the principles of textual criticism the translator has chosen to guide him.

The translators of NWT have adopted—as well as invented—certain principles whereby they have chosen a reading not found in their basic Greek text or in *any* Greek text. Unfortunately, the Foreword has not set these principles down in some clear fashion. They must be garnered from the Foreword, the body of the translation, footnotes, and the Appendix.

Explicit Principles

Of the few statements in NWT from which definite principles may be drawn, these may be set forth. The first can be termed a principle of non-interpolation: "We refuse to add anything to God's written Word."[22] At first glance one might regard this as a principle restricted to the translation itself and having nothing at all to do with the text underlying the NWT. But inasmuch as NWT claims to be a literal translation of the Greek text, any addition to the translation implies warrant for that addition in the text itself. It is not the investigator's intention at this point to discuss whether or not NWT has been faithful to this principle.

A second principle, and ostensibly one pertaining almost exclusively to translating, is that of rendering one Greek word by the same English word insofar as the context permits.[23] Textually, this indicates to the reader that one particular Greek word is in view and provides a limited type of concordance.

Finally, NWT exhibits the very important textual principle of weighing

---

22. Ibid., p. 771.
23. Ibid., p. 9.

rather than counting manuscripts. This is seen, for example, in the omission of Mark 16:9ff. from the main body of the text. Following, of course, their Westcott and Hort printed edition, NWT translators concur with them that quality of evidence is to be preferred. Other passages omitted on the basis of this principle are Luke 23:34, John 7:53–8:11, Acts 8:37, and I John 5:7-8.

Implicit and Inferential Principles

Whether or not a principle is in reality an implication or an inference may border upon the fine line of subjective opinion. Therefore, no dogmatic attempt will be made to determine whether the following principles are implied by NWT or inferred by the investigator. This writer's opinion, however, is that they are primarily inferential, since it is not likely that NWT meant to present by implication in the text or footnotes a full account of their textual method. The Foreword of NWT is detailed enough to have included these implied or inferred principles.

Interpolation. As a principle of textual criticism interpolation has little to commend itself for profitable use. For two reasons this is true. In the first place, the translator or textual critic has before him a critical edition or editions of the New Testament, and his task is to *exclude*—an antonym of ''interpolate''—that which is not genuine. Secondly, addition to the text is perhaps the greatest source of variant readings in the New Testament. Says Caspar René Gregory:

> What unintentional errors and faults did not do in eleven centuries they certainly could not have done in either one of the twelve periods of a century and a half before the eleven centuries. The classes of text in the New Testament are solely the result of arbitrary, that is, willed action.[24]

A translation should avoid adding any word in its text where the Greek text already has a well-attested reading.

That NWT exhibits interpolation to some degree throughout the New Testament the following examples will be sufficient to demonstrate. Mark 2:4 reads, ''But not being able to bring him right to Jesus on account of the crowd. . . .''[25] The text of Westcott and Hort reads αὐτῷ—as do apparently *all* manuscript witnesses, for no variant is cited—and not ''Jesus.'' Now it is apparent that to have translated ''to bring him right to him'' would

---

24. Caspar René Gregory, *The Canon and Text of the New Testament,* p. 503.
25. The *New World Translation of the Holy Scriptures,* 1961 edition, reads ''[Jesus].''

have been a bit awkward. But the difficulty would not have arisen had NWT omitted the practice of interpolation, because here is an example where one interpolation led to a second. The Greek of the verse actually reads, καὶ μὴ δυνάμενοι προσενέγκαι αὐτῷ διὰ τὸν ὄχλον. NWT has not only substituted "Jesus" for αὐτῷ but has inserted αὐτόν into the text where Mark omitted it for the sake of brachylogy. "Jesus" is marked by a footnote saying, "Literally, 'him.' "[26]

Just above this verse in 1:45 "Jesus" is substituted for αὐτόν with a footnote reading, "Literally, 'he.' "[27] Mark 6:14 is similarly rendered, in that NWT has "the name of Jesus" for the Greek τὸ ὄνομα αὐτοῦ. The note at the bottom of the page states, "Literally, 'for his name.' "[28]

When a translation announces that it is going to be a literal one concerning the use and translation of something so small—but not insignificant—as the Greek article, as NWT does in its Appendix on John 1:1, the reader is given the impression that nothing extraneous shall find inclusion in the work. This impression issues also from the Foreword of NWT itself and from Jehovah's Witnesses whom this investigator has encountered. The impression one receives from NWT is that interpolation has no place in it. Perhaps nowhere else in NWT is interpolation better illustrated than in Hebrews 12:22-24.

The passage reads as follows with the exception of brackets which have been inserted by this investigator in order to indicate words not found in the Greek:

> But you have approached a mount Zion and a city of [the] living God, heavenly Jerusalem, and myriads of angels, in general assembly, and [the] congregation of [the] firstborn who have been enrolled in [the] heavens, and God [the] Judge of all, and [the] spiritual [lives] of righteous ones who have been made perfect, [the] mediator of a new covenant, and [the] blood of sprinkling which speaks in a better way than Abel's blood.

It seems to this writer that the very least that could have been done would have been either the bracketing or the italicizing of these articles. Especially is this so in that NWT emphasizes the anarthrous character of "a mount

---

26. *New World Translation,* p. 130.
27. Ibid.
28. Ibid., p. 143.

Zion,'' ''a city,'' and ''a new covenant.''[29] Further incongruity is added by
a footnote after ''lives'' which reads, ''Literally, '(the) spirits.' ''[30] Here,
as will be demonstrated elsewhere, there is, on the one hand, a confusing of
an anarthrous word with the idea of indefiniteness, and, on the other hand,
an equating of definiteness with the presence of the article. This passage
clearly manifests arbitrary interpolation on the part of the NWT translators.
A more abundant manifestation of this principle applying to θεός will be
discussed in chapter 4.

The capstone of the interpolation principle is the wholesale addition of the
Divine Name ''Jehovah'' to the pages of the New Testament, interpolation
for which there exists no acceptable manuscript evidence whatsoever. Chapter 3 will deal exclusively with this matter; mention alone is made at this
point to illustrate further the interpolative principle as it is actually practiced
by the NWT translators.

The so-called Trinitarian Benediction of II Corinthians 13:14 furnishes
another example of NWT interpolation. The Greek text, Ἡ χάρις τοῦ
κυρίου Ἰησοῦ χριστοῦ καὶ ἡ ἀγάπη τοῦ θεοῦ καὶ ἡ κοινωνία τοῦ
ἁγίου πνεύματος μετὰ πάντων ὑμῶν, is rendered, ''The undeserved
kindness of the Lord Jesus Christ and the love of God and the sharing in the
holy spirit be with all of YOU.'' One notices immediately that the genitive
phrases in the original, ''of the Lord Jesus,'' ''of God,'' and ''of the the
Holy Spirit,'' are parallel; but NWT disrupts this coextensive grammatical
construction by ''the sharing in the holy spirit.'' This disruption has apparently been justified by translating κοινωνία as ''sharing'' and thus calling
forth the idiomatic ''sharing *in*.'' The parity of the genitives is broken and
the impersonality of ''the holy spirit'' emphasized, misleading the English
reader into assuming that behind the text of NWT lie the Greek prepositions
or constructions for ''of'' and ''in.''

A final example of NWT employment of interpolation is the insertion of
''Son'' in brackets in Acts 20:28. Paul tells the presbyters from Ephesus that
the Holy Spirit has appointed them ''to shepherd the congregation of God,
which he purchased with the blood of his own [Son].'' Footnote ''a'' refers
the reader to an ''Appendix under Acts 20:28.'' This Appendix discusses the
difficulty of the thought that God's blood was spilled on the cross and

---

29. The 1961 edition of the whole Bible has only ''the'' bracketed in this same passage.
30. *New World Translation*, p. 659.

presents Weymouth's explanation in support of Knapp's conjecture that the autograph read τοῦ αἵματος τοῦ ἰδίου υἱοῦ. Then follows,

> We have retained the ℵ B reading of the articulate θεοῦ and have rendered the passage literally, adding "Son" in brackets after the ἰδίου to read: "the congregation of God, which he purchased with the blood of his own [Son]."[31]

It is not germane to enter here into a discussion as to the correctness of this conjecture. The point to be made, however, is that NWT has taken up a conjecture into the text, even though bracketed, and this action was prompted to some degree by a "preferred religious view."[32] That view, of course, is that Jesus Christ is not to be identified with God.

Rationalism. In the discipline of textual criticism reason is a *sine qua non.* There is no place for shallow thinking. Yet reason is not the ultimate criterion for the acceptance of a particular reading. To construct a text or produce a translation with human reason as ultimate, and not the Word of God itself according to the *analogia fidei,* is to cast one's lot with the Greek philosopher Parmenides. For, "according to Parmenides only that can exist which man is able to penetrate by means of his logical function."[33] *Logical thinking* which confesses *no other basis* for truth is *rationalism.* As such, it is destructive to the Christian faith's confession of *revelation* and *mystery.*

The NWT illustrates technically and Witnesses illustrate practically that there can be no place in the Jehovah Witness *Weltanschauung* for the Christian doctrine of the Trinity. The primary reason for its denial is its utter irrationality. This principle of rationalism is best demonstrated in the Appendix to John 1:1.[34] NWT renders the verse, "and the Word was a god." To have translated "the Word was God" would indicate that

> . . . the Word was the God with whom the Word was said to be. *This is unreasonable;* for how can the Word be with the God and at the same time be that same God?[35] [italics supplied]

It is to be observed that the line of reasoning is not whether or not Jesus Christ *can* be deity, or if the Scriptures teach the tri-unity of the Godhead;

31. Ibid., p. 778.
32. See p. 6 of the NWT Foreword, where such views are condemned.
33. C. Van Til, *Christianity in Conflict,* I, 47.
34. See chapters 4 and 5 for a detailed discussion of this verse.
35. *New World Translation,* p. 774.

rather, it is an *a priori* rationalism that is the final court of appeal. The NWT treatment of the impersonality of the Holy Spirit, also a product of this criterion, will be discussed in chapter 5.

Conclusion

In this chapter the investigator has endeavored to go behind the mere product of the Watchtower Bible and Tract Society—the English translation—for he is thoroughly convinced that one cannot scribe a dichotomy between a translation and those who produce it. As Rudolph Bultmann asks in a brief article in *Glauben und Verstehen, "Ist voraussetzungslose Exegese möglich?"* and concludes by answering in the negative, so also a Bible translation is not produced apart from the translators' presuppositions.[36] The apparent vogue of the twentieth century claims that translators are simply scholars who ply their trade in neutral fashion and remain unaffected by doctrinal, theological, and philosophical considerations. The NWT refutes this notion, even on the basis of the brief excursion into the translation in this chapter.

No positive assertion can be made regarding academic qualifications of the NWT translators. Nor are their assertions about the weaknesses and prejudices of foregoing English versions and their asseverations about the unbiased, correct character of NWT overwhelming. Everyone, however, will join in commending the translators for setting forth such a noble aim as to provide an unbiased, modern, consistent, and literal translation.

It already has been mentioned that the Greek text chosen as the basis for the work was that of Westcott and Hort. Well-known by itself, this text served as the basis for the English Revised and American Standard Versions. The NWT committee also availed itself of other good critical Greek editions and, unfortunately, to a number of Hebrew versions. The use of the latter is singularly amazing, especially to anyone critically trained in New Testament studies. The table on page 101 indicates the lateness of these translations; their tardiness alone ought to have been sufficient argument against their employment in reconstructing the text of the New Testament.

Special citation for merit goes to NWT for its attempt to list manuscript

---

36. Rudolph Bultmann, *Glauben und Verstehen,* Dritte Band, 1960, pp. 142-150 (trans., "Is Exegesis without Presuppositions Possible?").

support for variant readings and for the high view of inspiration enunciated in the Foreword.

The few textual principles discussed were garnered, not without difficulty, from the Foreword, Appendix, and body of the translation. It may be demonstrated that at times each was used inconsistently. Perhaps the most objectionable—and the most dangerous—principle manifested is that of rationalism. The Witnesses' denunciation of unbelieving science and theological liberalism for their antisupernaturalistic rationalism is possibly equaled *only* by the rationalistic criterion of the Witnesses themselves.

The following chapter concerns itself with the Divine Name and is, therefore, a development of the topic briefly discussed herein, the Hebrew translations.

Chapter 3

THE DIVINE NAME

The singular importance of the Divine Name for the Jehovah's Witnesses is to be seen in the appellation they have chosen for themselves: they are witnesses for *Jehovah*. The strict monotheism of the group is further emphasized by this Divine Name when it is realized that one is not to be content with the mere use of the name "God" with its widespread popularity and corresponding ambiguity, but that one must press for the employment of the divinely revealed name of the one true GOD, JEHOVAH.

All such desire to set off the true God of Christianity from the myriads of "gods" worshiped in the world today finds welcome reception among orthodox Christians. The ambiguity of the term "God" in the nebulous theologies and existential philosophies that pervade religious thinking increases the demands upon the true Christian to define God in the most meaningful terms possible.

In his *By What Standard?* Rushdoony captures the signal importance of God's absolute differentiation from all other concepts of "God" when he says:

> While Scripture gives many titles to God, it records one name; the titles constitute man's recognition, in terms of a theophany usually, of a particular aspect of His being; the name Yahweh or Jehovah, is God's self-identification and constitutes His revelation of His nature and being. God declared Himself to be I AM THAT I AM, or HE WHO IS, the self-sufficient, self-contained, and absolutely sovereign and independent God. In declaring Himself to be Yahweh, God plainly declared, I do not explain myself, nor can I explain myself except in terms of My own being and self-sufficiency, I AM THAT I AM, HE WHO IS. . . . Not only must we assert that Christian orthodoxy is impossible without "the notion of the self-contained God" but that all things are impossible and inexplicable apart from Him.[1]

Christians, then, will not be reticent to commend Jehovah's Witnesses and

---

1. Rousas J. Rushdoony, *By What Standard?*, pp. 151-52.

19

NWT for enunciating this absolute differentiation between God and the many gods of this world. This commendation, however, is not to be taken so as to imply that their unitarian view of God is acceptable. But now it is incumbent to note what NWT has to say about the Divine Name and what results stem from this.

I. *The Foreword of NWT*

Of the thirty-three pages comprising the Foreword of NWT, twenty-four, or about two-thirds, are taken up with the discussion of the Divine Name. In the *New World Translation of the Holy Scriptures,* the complete Bible published in one volume in 1961, this entire Foreword is missing. Hence, the reader without knowledge of Witness dogmatics is left without explanation for the presence of "Jehovah" in the New Testament.

The NWT contention in its discussion of the Divine Name begins thus. One striking fact so patent about the extant manuscripts of the original Greek text and also of so many versions, both ancient and modern, is the absence of the Divine Name. That name was represented in the Hebrew Scriptures by the tetragrammaton written יהוה, occurring 6,823 times. Although the exact pronunciation of the name is unknown today, its most popular vocalization is "Jehovah."[2]

Since the Christian Greek Scriptures were an inspired addition, the Foreword continues, to the sacred Hebrew Scriptures, it seems grossly inconsistent that this name should disappear from the Greek text, especially when the Apostle James addressed the other apostles and disciples in Jerusalem about the year A.D. 50, saying:

> "Symeon has related thoroughly how God for the first time turned his attention to the nations to take out of them a people for his name" (Acts 15:14). Then in support James made a quotation from the Hebrew Scriptures where the divine name occurs twice. If Christians are to be a people for God's name, why should his name, represented by the tetragrammaton, be abolished from the Christian Greek Scriptures?[3]

"The usual traditional explanation for this no longer holds." For a long time it was thought that the reason for this absence of the Divine Name in

---

2. *New World Translation,* p. 10.
3. Ibid., p. 11.

extant manuscripts was the corresponding absence of it in the Septuagint.[4] This line of thinking, to be sure, was based upon the *copies* of the LXX found in the great manuscripts of the fourth and fifth centuries A.D. In these manuscripts—Codices Vaticanus, Sinaiticus, Alexandrinus, and Ambrosianus—God's name is rendered by the Greek words ΚΥΡΙΟΣ, "with or without the definite article," and ΘΕΟΣ. "This namelessness," write the translators of the NWT, "was viewed as an aid to teaching monotheism."[5]

NWT continues. The recently found remains of a papyrus roll of the LXX containing the second half of Deuteronomy have flatly disproved this popular theory. Dated by authorities to have been written in the second or first century B.C., the fragments of this papyrus *nowhere* show that either ΚΥΡΙΟΣ or ΘΕΟΣ was used instead of the tetragrammaton. This proves that

> . . . the original LXX did contain the divine name wherever it occurred in the Hebrew original. Considering it a sacrilege to use some substitute as *ky´·ri·os* or *the·os´*, *the scribes inserted the tetrgrammaton (* יהוה *) at its proper place in the Greek version text.*[6]

So important is this papyrus, technically designated P. Fouad 266, that NWT devotes two pages of the Foreword to photographic reproduction of some of its fragments.[7]

Did then Jesus and the disciples, the writers of the Christian Greek Scriptures, have copies available of the LXX with the Divine Name written in the tetragrammaton form, the translators ask? "Yes! The tetragrammaton

---

4. Hereinafter referred to as LXX.

5. *New World Translation*, p. 11.

6. Ibid., pp. 11-12.

7. Footnote "a" on page 12 of the Foreword reads: "The papyrus belongs to the Société Royale de Paprologie du Caire. It bears the Inventory Number 266, and forms part of the collection of Fouad Papyri, of which Nos. 1-89 were published in 1939 in one volume (*P. Fouad I*, 1939). The nearest parallel in date to P. Fouad Inv. No. 266 is P. Rylands iii. 458, of the 2nd century B.C., which also contains fragments of the second half of Deuteronomy; but its scanty remains unfortunately preserve no use of the divine name or its equivalent." The importance of this footnote is not so much in its content as in the fact that it is a verbatim quotation from W. D. Waddell's "The Tetragrammaton in the LXX" in the *Journal of Theological Studies* XLV, 158-61, written in 1944. *NWT does not place this paragraph in quotation marks or cite its source.* (Several attempts at securing clear copies of these originals for inclusion here have proved unsuccessful.)

persisted in copies of LXX for centuries after Christ and his apostles."[8]

Further evidence is adduced by citing Jerome in his *Prologus Galeatus*, where he prefaces the books of Samuel and Malachi by saying, "We find the four-lettered name of God (i.e., יהוה) in certain Greek volumes even to this day expressed in the ancient letters."[9] And in his twenty-fifth letter to Marcella, which he penned at Rome in the year 384, he discusses the ten names of God and states:

> The ninth [name of God] is a tetragrammaton, which they considered ἀνεκφώνητον [an·ek·pho´ne·ton], that is, unspeakable, which is written with these letters, Iod, He, Vau, He. Which certain ignorant ones, because of the similarity of the characters, when they would find them in Greek books, were accustomed to pronounce Pi Pi.[10]

According to NWT the evidence is incontrovertible, and one matter is now certain: whether Jesus and the disciples read Scripture in Aramaic or Greek, they would find the Divine Name in its tetragrammaton form.

One must now query whether Jesus followed the traditional Jewish custom of the day and vocalized *Adonai* for the tetragrammaton. The answer is simple if one accepts NWT reasoning: "Not if Jesus followed his usual disregard for the unscriptural traditions followed by the Jewish scribes."[11] For Jesus taught with authority and not as the scribes. In John 17:6, 26, he says: "I have made your name manifest to the men you gave me out of the world.. . . I have made your name known to them and will make it known."[12] Why even the Jewish Talmud, continues the Foreword, accuses Jesus of performing miracles by pronouncing the Divine Name. This in itself indirectly proves that he vocalized the tetragrammaton.[13]

The line of argument to this point has been simply groundwork, an attempt to establish solidly a basis upon which the crucial superstructure might find support:

> The question now before us is: Did Jesus' inspired disciples use the divine name in their writings? That is, Did God's name appear in the

8. Ibid.
9. Ibid., p. 16.
10. Ibid.
11. Ibid.
12. Ibid., pp. 338, 340.
13. Ibid., p. 17.

original writings of the Christian Greek Scriptures? We have basis for answering Yes.[14]

"In recent years some have claimed that Matthew's gospel account was at first written in Hebrew rather than in its kindred language, the Aramaic." Now, it is contended by some that Matthew and other early Christians intended this writing to take its place as the last book of the Hebrew canon. At that time a canon of Christian Greek Scriptures was not contemplated. Jerome is again cited in partial support of this hypothesis:

> Matthew, who is also Levi, and who from a publican came to be an Apostle, first of all the Evangelists, composed a Gospel of Christ in Judaea in the Hebrew language and characters, for the benefit of those of the circumcision who had believed. Who translated it into Greek is not sufficiently ascertained. Furthermore, the Hebrew itself is preserved to this day in the library at Caesarea which the martyr Pamphilus so diligently collected. I also was allowed by the Nazarenes who use this volume in the Syrian city of Beroea to copy it. In which it is to be remarked that, wherever the Evangelist makes use of the testimonies of the old Scripture, he does not follow the authority of the seventy translators, but of the Hebrew.[15]

More than one hundred times did Matthew quote from the Hebrew Scriptures, and "where these quotations included the Divine Name, he would be obliged faithfully to include the tetragrammaton in his Hebrew gospel account."[16]

How this relates to the other writers of the Christian Greek Scriptures is explained thus:

> But all the writers of the Christian Greek Scriptures quoted from the Hebrew Scriptures or from the LXX at verses where the Name appears, and they could follow the style then true of copies of the LXX by using the tetragrammaton in their Greek writings.[17]

In this fashion the gamut of the New Testament is run and the tetragrammaton is conclusively "discovered" to have been part of the autographa.

One further question begs to be asked by any thoughtful reader: Why is there no extant manuscript of the New Testament containing the tetragram-

14. Ibid.
15. Ibid.
16. Ibid.
17. Ibid., p. 18.

maton? And by no means have the NWT translators been remiss in supplying an answer to this desideratum:

> The evidence is, therefore, that the original text of the Christian Greek Scriptures has been tampered with, the same as the text of the LXX has been. And, at least from the 3d century A.D. onward, the divine name in tetragrammaton form has been eliminated from the text by copyists who did not understand or appreciate the divine name or who developed an aversion to it, possibly under the influence of anti-Semitism. In place of it they substituted the words *ky·ri·os* (usually translated "the Lord") and *the·os,* meaning "God."[18]

And *since*—not "if"—such has been the case, the modern translator is duty bound to restore the name of Jehovah to the text of the New Testament, the NWT argument runs.

Appendix to Matthew 1:20

Of the numerous appendices in the back of NWT the one appended to Matthew 1:20 is entitled "Jehovah's." It lists as a concordance every place in the NWT where the translators have substituted "Jehovah" for the Greek *Kyrios* or *Theos.* In the body of NWT, "Jehovah" has been inserted 237 times, and "Jah"—the abbreviated form—four times. The lower margin or apparatus contains Jehovah 72 times. These were not considered to be genuine enough to be taken up into the text. The total number of times, then, that the Divine Name appears in the body of the translation is 241.[19]

Where Jehovah appears, there is a footnote which gives the Greek reading of *Kyrios* or *Theos* and the chief manuscript evidence supporting it. Usually, this evidence consists of the uncials A B ℵ C D and the Latin, Syria, and Coptic Versions.

Medieval Hebrew Translations of the New Testament

In view of the "conclusive" evidence,

> What is the modern translator to do? Is he justified, yes, authorized, to enter the divine name into a translation of the Christian Greek Scrip-

---

18. Ibid. One observes here, in an aside, that NWT translators have used "anti-Semitism" for "anti-Jewishness." This imprecise use of terminology is widespread still. *Real* anti-Semitism includes an animus against Arabs.

19. For the listing of "Jehovah's" see pages 759-62 of the NWT.

tures? Every Greek reader must confess that in the LXX the Greek words *ky·ri·os* and *the·os* have been used to crowd out the distinctive name of the Supreme Deity.

Then it is stated that all comprehensive Greek-English lexicons agree that these two Greek words have been employed as equivalents for the Divine Name. Therefore,

> . . . the modern translator is warranted in using the divine name as an equivalent of those two Greek words, that is, at places where Matthew, etc., quote verses, passages and expressions from the Hebrew Scriptures or from the LXX where the divine name occurs.[20]

Since insertion of the name has been justified in the minds of NWT translators, the transition from the sole use of Greek manuscripts to Hebrew translations of the New Testament must likewise be seen to be justified.

On page 101 of this thesis a table of these Hebrew translations is given. The earliest, dated in the year 1385, and designated by NWT as J[2], marked the inception of many translations of parts or all of the New Testament into "the ancient classical Hebrew." The total number of appearances of the sacred tetragrammaton in the nineteen Hebrew versions available to NWT is 307. "These have thus restored the divine name to the inspired Christian Scriptures."[21]

Immediately, one notices that NWT substitutes Jehovah 237 times in the text and "Jah," its abbreviation, four times, sixty-six times fewer than the total number in the versions cited. The grave question raised is, "How is a modern translator to know or determine when to render the Greek words κύριος and θεός into the divine name in his version?" The solution proffered is thus:

> By determining where the inspired Christian writers have quoted from the Hebrew Scriptures. Then he must refer back to the original to locate whether the divine name appears there. This way he can determine the identity to give to *ky·ri·os* and *the·os* and he can then clothe them with personality.[22]

The translators, realizing that the time has come for restoring the Divine

---

20. Ibid., p. 19.
21. Ibid., p. 20.
22. Ibid.

Name, have followed this procedure in rendering their version. Also, realizing the danger of overstepping the limits of a translator and moving into the field of exegesis,

> . . . we have looked for some agreement with us by the Hebrew versions we consulted to confirm our own rendering. Thus, out of the 237 times that we have rendered the divine name in the body of our version there are only two instances where we have no support or agreement from any of the Hebrew versions. [23]

From these admissions the NWT awareness of subjectivism is apparent; and a concerted attempt has been made to be objective and to substantiate the insertions with tangible textual support.

Although *The Emphatic Diaglott,* issued in 1864 as an interlinear English/ Greek version based on Griesbach's text, was the first American translation to insert the name Jehovah into the English text, the *New World Translation* is the version having inserted Jehovah that has commended itself to more people and has made the greatest impact. The translators are convinced that "no reasonable mind can find Scriptural objection" to their treatment of the text in this fashion. Instead, it is said that readers who become familiar with NWT "will rejoice over the added clearness it imparts to many scriptures not distinctly discerned before." [24]

II. *Vocalization of the Divine Name*

In the preceding portion of this chapter in which was presented the NWT Foreword as it attempted to justify the "restoration" of the Divine Name, there is no questioning of the pronunciation of "Jehovah" or, more basically, vocalization of the tetragrammaton itself. [25] If the Witnesses are to be a people of God's name, and if His name had been preserved in the Greek autographa in ancient Hebrew letters, then it seems reasonable to expect that pronunciation of His name would be preserved also.

The importance of vowels must be squarely faced, especially by the Witnesses, who vociferate their status as witnesses for Jehovah God. A cursory perusal of any Hebrew lexicon soon demonstrates that one set of radicals can admit of widely divergent meanings. For example, the radi-

---

23. Ibid.
24. Ibid., p. 25.
25. The tetragrammaton also is spoken of as the "ineffable sacrosanct."

cals שַׁד when pointed שֵׁד mean "teat," when שֵׁד mean "demon,"
when שֹׁד, "breast" or "violence." If it would be an impropriety to
mispronounce someone's name or to call a "breast" a "demon," then how
much more of an impropriety to vocalize incorrectly the name of the true
God?

In this section will be treated the "ineffable sacrosanct" in the LXX,
prohibition and the name, both leading up to the pronunciation of the name.

The Tetragrammaton in the LXX

The contention by the NWT translators that the autographa of the LXX
contained the tetragrammaton solely has been presented as it was set forth in
the Foreword of that version. Admittedly on every hand, if the autographa
were extant and able to be inspected, this matter would be settled with the
utmost expediency. But, as is the case with the autographs of the New
Testament, the original manuscripts of LXX long ago perished. In all candor
the NWT translators ought to admit that their line of reasoning is held
together by more dogmatism than fact, by more conjecture than textual
evidence.

Evidence in support of NWT contention. One statement preserved in the
works of the third-century Church Father Origen supports to some extent the
position adopted by NWT. Commenting on Psalm 2, Origen states:

Καὶ ἐν τοῖς ἀκριβεστάτοις δὲ τῶν ἀντιγράφων Ἑβραίοις χαρακ-
τῆρσιν κεῖται τὸ ὄνομα Ἑβραικοῖς δὲ οὐ τοῖς νῦν ἀλλὰ τοῖς
ἀρχαιοτάτοις.[26]

Translation: "Now in the most exact copies the name is situated in Hebrew
characters, though not in current but in the most ancient ones." Swete then
comments that "the most exact copies" to which Origin alludes must be
those of Aquila's version of the LXX. For, he continues, there is no reason to
suppose that any of the copyists of the LXX version stemming from Alex-
andria ever hesitated writing ὁ Ks or Ks for יהוה.[27]

In this same vein Waddell says that the Cairo palimpsests of parts of III and
IV Kings corroborates fully Origen's statement quoted above.[28]

---

26. Henry B. Swete, *An Introduction to the Old Testament in Greek*, p. 39.
27. Ibid.
28. W. D. Waddell, *Journal of Theological Studies* XLV (1944), p. 158.

Thus alongside the citation by the NWT Foreword of Jerome's knowledge of the tetragrammaton in Greek manuscripts may be placed Origen, who preceded Jerome by two centuries. Going back another century to the work of Aquila itself, Swete remarks that a noticed difference between Aquila's version and the LXX is that the tetragrammaton is not transliterated nor is κύριος translated for it; it is written in archaic Hebrew letters: 𐤉𐤄𐤅𐤄 and not יהוה.[29]

While in the Aquila version the tetragrammaton was archaically written, it appears that κύριος was read for it. In adducing evidence to support this, Swete cites F. C. Burkitt:

> Mr. Burkitt acutely points out (p. 16) that 𐤉𐤄𐤅𐤄(and doubtless also πιπι) was read as κύριος, since in one place in the Aquila fragments there was no room to write the Hebrew characters, "instead of οἴκῳ 𐤉𐤄𐤅𐤄 we find οἴκῳ κῦ."[30]

The rule, then, for the Aquila version was that the Divine Name should be preserved in its four-letter form. Translating it by κύριος was an exception.

In view of this combined testimony, there is some evidence to support the NWT Foreword when it alleges that Jesus and His disciples *might* have had copies of the LXX at hand containing the tetragrammaton.

Evidence against NWT contention. Contrary evidence might best begin with the latter issue, the version of Aquila. For to say that his version, which is dated in the first quarter of the second century of the Christian era, contained the Divine Name in ancient Hebrew characters is not to establish that such was the practice of all copyists who worked with the Greek Old Testament. In other words, can or must Aquila's version be normative?

In the opinion of the present investigator the answer to this question is clearly, No. Würthwein, discussing "later Greek translations," states concerning Aquila and his version:

> . . . from Sinope in Pontus, was a proselyte and, according to Jewish tradition, a pupil of Rabbi Akiba, in whose spirit he produced a slavishly literal translation. As he carried the principle of literal accuracy to the absurd point at which the intelligibility of the text suffered, he frequently produced a version which did not sound at all like Greek, although his vocabulary reveals that he had a good knowledge of the

---

29. Swete, *An Introduction to the Old Testament in Greek*, p. 39.
30. Ibid., p. 40.

language. But it was just this ruthless adherence to the text, and its rather precious quality, as for example in its use of similar sounding words, which endeared his work to his Jewish contemporaries, and his version thus enjoyed considerable popularity among the Jews.[31]

In light of this knowledge alone one must conclude the precariousness of alleging that the presence of the tetragrammaton in Aquila implies—even less proves—the same presence in the autographs of the LXX, which were produced some three hundred years earlier.[32] Also, Aquila could not have completed his version before *ca*. A.D. 130, *many* years after the completion of all—or at least most—of the NT writings. Thus, NWT infers from a *later* work by extrapolation backwards that NT writers *in fact* had a LXX with Hebraic entries for the tetragrammaton.

Though the *possibility* of the latter must be conceded, there is no hard evidence to justify NWT dogmatism on behalf of a Jehovah's Witness prior religious view.

One more piece of evidence contrary to NWT contention shall be adduced, and consideration of it should be made in view of Papyrus Fouad 266.

---

31. Ernst Würthwein, *The Text of the Old Testament*, pp. 137f.

32. Further elucidation of Aquila's style comes from a leading LXX scholar, Alfred Rahlfs: ". . . Aquila . . . did not shrink from perpetrating the most appalling outrages to the whole essence of the Greek language. We are provided in the very first verse of the Bible with a classical example of his translating. The LXX has rendered it into correct and good Greek by ἐν ἀρχῇ ἐποίησεν ὁ θεὸς τὸν οὐρανὸν καὶ τὴν γῆν. This translation was, however, very far from being accurate enough for Aquila's tastes. The etymology of the Hebrew רֵאשִׁית did not find expression in ἀρχή; Aquila, however, aimed at providing a rendering of all Hebrew derivatives which should be accurate, even in regard to etymology. He therefore translated רֵאשִׁית as a derivative of רֹאשׁ by κεφάλαιον, being a derivative of κεφαλή. It did not matter that the Greek word κεφάλαιον did not mean 'Beginning' but 'Chief point' or 'Sum,' etc. Neither was Aquila able to use the classical Greek word ἐποίησεν; for he used different renderings in Greek for different Hebrew words, and, consequently, ποιεῖν being to him the equivalent of עָשָׂה, he sought for another translation for בָּרָא, and this he found in κτίζειν, a word already frequently used in the LXX to render בָּרָא. The next word in the LXX was ὁ θεός= אֱלֹהִים; Aquila omitted the article, his reason being that it was not there in the Hebrew text. Finally, there came in the LXX the words τὸν οὐρανὸν καὶ τὴν γῆν. Aquila, in order to have a special Greek rendering even for אֵת, wrote σὺν τὸν οὐρανὸν καὶ σὺν τὴν γῆν. At this point he was plainly influenced by his teacher Akiba, who, as has been mentioned above, had taken אֵת in this context as meaning 'with.' All the same, in order to contradict previous inaccurate statements of the fact, it needs emphasizing that Aquila does not in every case render אֵת by σύν, but only on occasions when in the Hebrew text אֵת is followed by the article; should, however, a Hebrew word have no article preceding it, as, for example, in the case of a status constructus, or of a proper name, then Aquila translates אֵת by the Greek article." Alfred Rahlfs, *Septuaginta*, I, p. XXV.

Among the manuscripts found in the Qumran region beginning in 1947 is the Leviticus Scroll Fragment 4 Q LXX Lev.[a]. Dated as having been written around 100 B.C., it contains Leviticus 26:2-16. The present writer observed this manuscript on display at the University of Pennsylvania Museum in 1965, where it was featured along with other Dead Sea Scroll materials. A statement appended to the fragment read, ". . . this fragment is now the oldest copy of the Septuagint." This fragment produces the crux for the NWT contention because this Leviticus portion contains verses which in the Hebrew Massoretic text have the Divine Name in tetragrammaton form. Verses two and thirteen have the Divine Name once each and in neither instance did יהוה or ᴣ꓄ᴣ꓄ appear. The copyist maintained his usage of the Greek language throughout.

Conclusion. This treatment of the LXX has not attempted to be exhaustive, and there exists additional evidence, to be sure, that might be used pro and con.[33] One may conclude that NWT dogmatism has been to some extent emasculated by the foregoing evidence. And furthermore, the NWT position elicits a *petitio principii*—even if it were incontrovertibly established that the LXX originals employed the tetragrammaton in Hebrew characters, by no means would this establish such usage in the New Testament by the apostolic writer. Hence, the NWT circuitous reasoning by way of the LXX to New Testament autographa results in a futility.

Prohibitions Regarding the Divine Name

The sanctity which the name of God was accorded by both pre-Christian and post-Christian Jews is axiomatic. Among other testimony surviving to the present era is that of the first-century historian Flavius Josephus. Remarking on the general prohibition of vocalizing this name, he wrote:

Καὶ ὁ θεὸς αὐτῷ σημαίνει τὴν αὐτοῦ προσηγορίαν οὐ πρότεραν εἰς ἀνθρώπους παρελθοῦσαν, περὶ ἧς οὔ μοι θέμιτον εἰπεῖν.[34]

---

33. "Darüber hinaus ergibt sich aus der Art des Artikelgebrauchs bei κύριος dass in der ursprünglichen Septuaginta das Tetragramm nicht in hebräischen Buchstaben beibehalten, ebensowenig mit ἀδωναί umschrieben war und dass dafur nicht erst später κύριος substituiert worden ist." Worf W. G. Baudissin, *Kyrios als Gottesname im Judentum,* 1929, II, p. 15, cited by W. D. Waddell, op. cit., p. 159. Translation: "Further, there results from the manner of usage of the article with κύριος that in the original Septuagint the tetragram was not retained in Hebrew letters, just as little was it rewritten with ἀδωναί, and for that not until later did κύριος become substituted" [i.e., for ἀδωναί]. Waddell argues against this statement.

34. Josephus, *Jewish Antiquities,* English translation by H. St. J. Thackeray, 1930, II, xii,

In a footnote he states that only the High Priest was allowed to pronounce the tetragrammaton. J. Z. Lauterbach, citing Rabbinic sources, supports Josephus by saying that "In the Temple, especially on the Day of Atonement, the Name was pronounced by the High Priest."[35] One further allowance was made: "Also at the final stage of a court trial for blasphemy the witnesses were allowed to pronounce the Name used by the blasphemer."[36]

The tangent issue as touches the NWT is the statement of the Foreword regarding this prohibition:

> Did Jesus follow the traditional Jewish custom of the day and read *A·do·nai* at such places out of fear of profaning the name and violating the Third Commandment (Exodus 20:7)?[37]

The assumed and stated answer, of course, is "Not if Jesus followed his usual disregard for the unscriptural traditions followed by the Jewish scribes."[38]

In the first place, the wording of the question is very subtle. To be sure, Jesus did not conduct His tenure upon earth in superstitious fear. In the second place, and admittedly drawing from the silence of the New Testament record, nowhere is Jesus' profanation of the Divine Name cited. In the opinion of this investigator the accusers of Jesus would not have overlooked such incriminating evidence, for at His trial He is accused of βλασφημία.

In the same paragraph NWT cites what appears to them as incontrovertible proof that Jesus pronounced the Name:

> In the hearing of his faithful apostles Jesus prayed to Jehovah God, saying: "I have made your name manifest to the men you gave me out of the world. . . . I have made your name known to them and will make it known." (John 17:6, 26)[39]

The clear implication of the Foreword is *that part of Jesus' mission to earth was to restore to the lips of men a Name that had hitherto had its pronuncia-*

4, 276, p. 284. Translation: "And God shows him [Moses] His name not formerly having come forth to men, concerning which [name] I am not permitted to speak."

35. J. Z. Lauterbach, "Substitutes for the Tetragrammaton," *American Academy for Jewish Research*, Proceedings, 1931, p. 39.

36. Ibid.

37. *New World Translation*, p. 16.

38. Ibid.

39. Ibid.

tion obscured and lost. The Witnesses show a defective knowledge of biblical theology at this point.

Geerhardus Vos, discussing the name of God in the Old Testament, says that the Bible usage of the word "name" differs considerably from current usage. "In the Bible the name is always more than a conventional sign. It expresses character or history." He further states that there is a threefold significance of the term "name" in Scripture in its religious connections: (1) It may express a divine attribute. For example, God is holy. But the adjective becomes a proper noun when the prophet speaks of God as "The Holy One of Israel"; (2) next, God's name may "stand abstractly and comprehensively for all that God has revealed concerning Himself"; and, (3) God's name may stand in a real way for God Himself. It becomes equivalent to God in theophany.[40]

Jesus, then, when having prayed that He made the Father's name known in the world, *was not indicating a philological concern,* but a theological one.[41]

Pronunciation of the Tetragrammaton

Greater impasse can be reached here than at any other point in this chapter, for the ages of antiquity have completely effaced the vowel pointing of an originally "pointless" Hebrew word. Since modern scholarship has not yet solved this enigma, one can perhaps do no better than turn to the opinion of one who wrote in the nineteenth century, Gustaf Oehler.

Oehler avers that Exodus 3:13-15 provides the decisiveness necessary for the pronunciation and grammatical explanation of the name. When Moses queries who it is who sends him to the people of Israel, God replies, אֶהְיֶה אֲשֶׁר אֶהְיֶה . "Thus shalt thou say to the children of Israel, Ehyeh has sent me unto you." In verse 15, "Thus shalt thou say, יהוה , the God of your fathers has sent me unto you," leads Oehler to conclude that the word יהוה is to be taken as a noun formed from the third person of the imperfect הָוָה , an older form of הָיָה . Hence, the tetragrammaton

---

40. Geerhardus Vos, *Biblical Theology,* 1959, pp. 76f.

41. In the Gospels there is frequently a euphemistic substitute for the name of God. Readily, one observes that the phrase "kingdom of heaven," especially in Matthew, is the best example of such usage. Parallel Gospel passages usually use "kingdom of God." In Luke 15:18-21, the prodigal son is recorded as having confessed his sinning against God and his father: "I sinned against heaven and against thee."

must be pointed יַהֲוָה (יַהֲוָה), or, what is not impossible, יַהֲוָה (יַהֲוָה).
The testimony of tradition produces Ἰαβέ, Samaritans; Ἀιά, Jews;ʼΙαωια,
Origen; – Ιαω, Diodorus; Ἰευώ, Sanchoniathon; Ἰαού, Clement of Alex-
andria; *Jaho,* Jerome; and *Jeve,* Joachin de Floris in the thirteenth century.[42]

The educated guesses are few in number, and the present prospects for
solving the mystery with finality do not appear to be impressive.

III. *The Real Issue: The Identification of Jesus with Jehovah*

In this the final section of the presentation of the Divine Name, the real
issue is reached. The writer is thoroughly convinced that the translators of
NWT were not merely intending to restore to the pages of the New Testament God's name, which name, it is alleged, was perhaps exscinded due to
anti-semitism or ignorance on the part of early Christian scribes. NWT has
introduced "Jehovah" into the Greek Scriptures for the sole purpose of
wiping out any vestige of Jesus Christ's identity with Jehovah. From the
Witnesses' standpoint the "ambiguous" employment of κύριος and θεός
in the Greek Scriptures would lend weight to trinitarians who assert the deity
of Christ.

No attempt will be made here to present a case for Christ's deity, since that
will form the substance of chapter 5. However, in connection with this
section there will be presented tables demonstrating the inconsistency of
NWT in not adhering to their stated principle on page 20 of the Foreword.
That principle dealt with how to determine where to insert Jehovah:

> By determining where the inspired Christian writers have quoted from
> the Hebrew Scripture. Then he must refer back to the original to locate
> whether the divine name appears there. This way he can determine the
> identity to give to κύριος and θεός.[43]

Secondly, herein will be passages which clearly show an identity of Jesus
with Jehovah *on the basis of text alone.* Again, no attempt will be made to
follow out the implications. The sole purpose of the investigator at this point
will be to demonstrate that the inspired Scriptures *textually* make Jesus and
Jehovah correlative in some way at these places. Then it will be shown that

---

42. Gustav F. Oehler, *Theology of the Old Testament,* p. 93.
43. *New World Translation,* p. 20.

NWT has manifestly departed from its stated principle in order to avoid this identification.

Inconsistent Application of Principle

The principle to have been followed by NWT has already been stated, and a check of its application has not been difficult. Table II on page 102 contains a listing of κύριος in the New Testament where the Old Testament reference behind it contains the tetragrammaton. It will be immediately evident that NWT has been faithful to its principle the majority of times—in fact about ninety-five percent faithful. In table III on page 103 θεός is similarly listed, and there, involving fewer entries, NWT has been fifty-six percent faithful to its principle. One is compelled to posit the question, Why did not NWT follow its principle 100 percent of the time? The question is a valid one and demands an answer. Table IV on page 104 lists by books the occurrences of "Jehovah" in the main text of NWT and shows the actual number of times that the tetragrammaton occurs in quotation behind κύριος and θεός. The totals are extremely worthy of study. According to Moulton and Geden the Divine Name appears only 50 times in passages quoted by New Testament writers. When one re-reads the Foreword of NWT and notes that in order to

> . . . avoid overstepping the bounds of a translator into the field of exegesis, we have tried to be most cautious about rendering the divine name, always carefully considering the Hebrew Scriptures,[44]

one must wonder how the translators can account for the 187 other times they have inserted Jehovah into the sacred text!

Textual Identification of Jesus with Jehovah

The investigator presents this section of the chapter firmly believing that here objectivity immeasurably dominates subjectivity. Therefore, meaningful conclusions—and vital conclusions—will pregnantly manifest themselves. The first passage has been selected to head the others because it stands as the clearest of them all.

I Peter 2:3. Εἰ ἐγεύσασθε ὅτι χρηστὸς ὁ κύριος. Westcott and Hort place this phrase in uncials in order to show it to be a quotation; Nestle places

---

44. Ibid.

it in heavy type for the same reason. Psalm 34:8a (33:9a in LXX) furnishes the source and reads γεύσασθε καὶ ἴδετε ὅτι χρηστὸς ὁ κύριος. The Massoretic text reads טַעֲמוּ וּרְאוּ כִּי-טוֹב יְהוָה . On the basis of NWT contentions that LXX retained the tetragrammaton, Psalm 34:8 would have read γεύσασθε καὶ ἴδετε ὅτι χρηστὸς 𐤉𐤄𐤅𐤄 [or יהוה]. Continuing on this contention, Peter would have written Εἰ ἐγεύσασθε ὅτι χρηστὸς 𐤉𐤄𐤅𐤄 or יהוה . Therefore, the translation of I Peter 2:3 in NWT could be expected to read, "providing YOU have tasted that Jehovah is kind." *But such is not the case in* NWT, which reads, "providing YOU have tasted that the Lord is kind." *Certainly there must be a footnote that elucidates for the reader this departure from the established principle he has read in the Foreword.* But one will search in vain for any relevant footnote—and NWT abounds in footnotes on each page.

Why is the fervor of the Witnesses to restore the Divine Name not evidenced in this passage whose lucidity must be admitted by all? The answer is found in the next verse. Peter continues, πρὸς ὃν προσερχόμενοι, λίθον ζῶντα, ὑπὸ ἀνθρώπων μὲν ἀποδεδοκιμασμένον παρὰ δὲ θεῷ ἐκλεκτὸν ἔντιμον. There is no possible way aside from sheer chicanery to circumvent the grammatical construction of this verse, for πρὸς ὃν can refer to *no one* but Jesus Christ. He alone is the One to whom the addressees of I Peter have come, the Living Stone, the One rejected by men. Is it any wonder then that NWT translates the verse with "Lord" instead of "Jehovah" and tacitly avoids any comment at all?[45]

---

45. After having pointed out this passage and its implications to a Jehovah's Witness who had accosted this investigator, the Witness answered in typical rationalistic fashion, "But do you think that Jesus and Jehovah God are really the same?" I then emphasized that such a question was irrelevant in view of the principle set forth for restoring "Jehovah" in the Foreword of NWT. The Witness refused to admit any inconsistency whatsoever. The following reply indicates the refusal to face squarely the issue elicited by this passage: "Yes, I Peter 2:3 is one of the verses where in the Greek text the word *Kyrios* or Lord occurs. However, it is not anarthrous *Kyrios* such as is used to represent the divine name Jehovah, that is, preceded by the definite article, the same as in the English text. So it is not in the list of those Hebrew versions where the word Jehovah occurs. If you will turn to page 762 of the appendix found in the *New World Translation of the Christian Greek Scriptures* you will find there a list of texts that you request, namely, those verses of the Christian Greek Scriptures where Hebrew versions do contain the name Jehovah, but in which verses the *New World Translation* does not present the name Jehovah in the main text, but only in the lower margin of the page." Watchtower Bible and Tract Society (personal letter, unsigned; New York, August 16, 1965). *I include this so that*

I Peter 3:15a. Here the Apostle Peter again quotes the Old Testament where the tetragrammaton is used. Westcott and Hort—the affirmed basic text of NWT— and Nestle read Peter's imperative: κύριον δὲ τὸν χριστὸν ἁγιάσατε ἐν ταῖς καρδίαις ὑμῶν. NWT translates it thus: "But sanctify the Christ as Lord[b] in YOUR hearts." It is passing strange that the translators could have overlooked this quotation (Isa. 8:13), where the Hebrew reads "sanctify" יהוה אֶת . The particle *'eth* denotes the accusative, the sign of the direct object. Hence, it is Jehovah God who is to be set apart. Peter, apparently following LXX, wrote κύριον δὲ τὸν χριστὸν ἁγιάσατε. He clearly places "Christ" in the accusative with, if you will, the tetragrammaton. Κύριον and τὸν χριστόν are separate only because the postpositive δέ cannot appear first in a sentence or clause.

There is a footnote to this part of verse 15. It reads:

> [b]Sanctify the Christ as Lord, א BAVgSyP; sanctify the Messiah our Lord, J[18]; sanctify the Lord God, Textus Receptus; sanctify Jehovah God, J[7, 8, 12-14, 16, 17] [46]

At best the data cited in this footnote are misleading. First, the evidence in favor of the text, though weighty enough by itself, should have been accompanied by *plerique* or *reliqui* or at least *permulti* to indicate further the status of this reading. Secondly, "sanctify the Messiah our Lord," which comes next, ought not to have preceded that of Textus Receptus, for it will be noted that J[18] is a Hebrew translation which was begun in the modern year of 1885! And thirdly, the final variant reading, "sanctify Jehovah God," found in seven medieval Hebrew translations, is a conflate reading based upon the great body of medieval manuscripts underlying Textus Receptus. The combined effect of all these citations upon the untrained reader may induce him to concude that the greater evidence favors "Jehovah God."

In keeping with the aim of the Foreword for an "honest" translation, this footnote ought to have included a candid acknowledgement of the presence

---

the reader can observe how the Society refuses to acknowledge that the divine tetragrammaton stands in the Hebrew behind the LXX which Peter cites.

The grossness of NWT inconsistency in *not* following their theory—that the tetragrammaton was represented in LXX by the *anarthrous* κύριος—they fail to tell the reader that in Aquila's LXX he used 𐤉𐤄𐤅𐤄 *interchangeably* with both κύριος *and* ὁ κύριος (cf., e.g., Ps. 91:5-10 [92:5-10 in most English versions], Swete, ibid., p. 38).

46. *New World Translation*, p. 679.

of the tetragrammaton. *As it now stands NWT is guilty of a flagrant violation of its dogmatically stated principle as touching the Divine Name.* Further evidence of not presenting *all* the facts is to be seen in the marginal reference in verse 14 to Isaiah 8:12 without referring the reader to 8:13 somewhere in verse 15 of Peter. Had this been done, the reader might have realized that "Jehovah" stands behind "Lord" and is placed in juxtaposition with "Christ." *Caveat emptor!*

John 19:37. This passage differs from the preceding two in that the Divine Name is not involved immediately but only mediately by way of being the antecedent. NWT reads, "And, again, a different scripture says: 'They will look upon the one whom they pierced.' " The Apostle John is quoting from Zechariah 12:10—which reference appears in the margin of NWT— and he sees its fulfillment in the thrusting of a Roman soldier's spear into the side of Jesus.

The Greek of John 19:37 is not identical with that of LXX but, according to a marginal note by Nestle, is similar to the Greek in Zechariah 12:10 of the versions of Aquila and Theodotion. Actually, this is of no consequence. The importance of the quotation is seen in that the antecedent of "the one" in the phrase "the one one whom they pierced" can be none other than Jehovah God.

As the matter stands in NWT, Jehovah is *not* seen to be the antecedent. The *New World Translation of the Holy Scriptures,* published in 1961 and containing the Old Testament as well as the "Christian Greek Scriptures," which are the subject of this dissertation, reads in Zechariah 12:10:

> And I will pour out upon the house of David and upon the inhabitants of Jerusalem the spirit of favor and entreaties, and they will certainly look to the One whom they pierced through, and they will certainly wail over him as in the wailing over an only [son]; and there will be a bitter lamentation over him as when there is bitter lamentation over the first-born [son].

In general the translation of this verse is acceptable. In one small, and insignificant point, however, the translators have erred greatly. The phrase, "and they will certainly look to the One whom they pierced through" reads in the King James Version and the American Standard Version, "and they shall look upon/unto me whom they have pierced." The American Standard used "unto" instead of "upon." The only real difference with NWT is the person to whom these "piercers" look. In agreement with its translation, NWT has the Revised Standard Version, whose rendering of the phrase under study is, "so that when they look on him whom they have pierced. . . ."

The LXX reads καὶ ἐπιβλέψονται πρός με ἀνθ᾽ ὧν κατωρχήσαντο and the Massoretic text, וְהִבִּיטוּ אֵלַי אֵת אֲשֶׁר־דָּקָרוּ , both supporting KJV and ASV. The basis for this peculiar variant found in NWT and RSV is apparently the reading of Zechariah 12:10 in a Greek version by Theodotion, a second-century A.D. Jewish proselyte. *This is not cited by NWT,* but it is placed in a footnote by RSV. The more difficult and better attested reading is that of the Massoretic text, "unto me," and it is readily seen that "to the One whom" could be a dogmatic correction on the part of a Jewish scribe who *knew* that Jehovah could not be "pierced through." And, if tradition be correct, Theodotion *was* a proselyte to Judaism and could have introduced such a variation.

Commenting on the apparent difficulty produced by this "piercing of Jehovah," C. F. Keil says:

> The suffix in אֵלַי (to *me*) refers to the speaker. This is *Jehovah,* according to ver. 1, the creator of the heaven and the earth. . . .It is true that we have not to think of a slaying of Jehovah, the creator of the heaven and the earth, but simply of the slaying of *Maleach* Jehovah, who, being of the same essence with Jehovah, became man in the person of Jesus Christ.[47]

The difficulty is really no difficulty at all when the biblical view of the Godhead is allowed to assert itself, which trinitarian doctrine the Witnesses reject with anathemas. In summary of this passage, it ought to be lucidly plain that—and, to use a phrase from the NWT Foreword—"a preferred religious view" provided the impetus for NWT's selecting a most poorly attested variant in Zechariah 12:10 in order to weaken the biblical presentation of the person of the Messiah of Jehovah. When one sees this passage applied to the Savior in John 19:37, there can, then, be no denying His identification *in some way* with Jehovah.

The several passages taken under discussion here by no means exhaust the list of those which serve to enhance further this Jesus/Jehovah identification.

---

47. C. F. Keil, *Biblical Commentary on the Old Testament,* vol. XXV, *The Twelve Minor Prophets,* pp. 387f.

Others might include (1) II Peter 3:9, 15, where NWT reads in verse 15 "the patience of our Lord" and refers this to Christ, and verse 9, where patience or longsuffering is ascribed to Jehovah; (2) Revelation 1:8 and 2:8, where Jehovah is Alpha and Omega and Jesus is First and Last, respectively; and, (3) Revelation 17:14; 19:16; and I Timothy 6:15, where Jehovah and Jesus Christ come under the appellation "King of Kings and Lord of Lords." A marginal reference in Nestle gives Daniel 2:47 and Deuteronomy 10:17 as the source of this phrase, and, upon reading each, one cannot deny that Jehovah is the One so depicted; and, (4) a comparison of Romans 14:10f. with Philippians 2:6-11; for in the latter Jesus Christ is said to have been given "the name which is above every name." Could there be any name above God's name itself? If in Isaiah 42:8 God states: "I am Jehovah; that is my name; and my glory I will not give to another," how can Jesus be named with *the* name par excellence unless He be identified in some way with Jehovah ontologically?

Conclusion

In this chapter the investigator has attempted to set forth fairly the Foreword of NWT regarding the Divine Name. It was contended on the part of NWT that, since Christians are to be a people for God's name, it is a strange matter not to find God's only real name on the pages of the Christian Greek Scriptures. Then, by working forward from the Hebrew Scriptures to the Septuagint and attempting to establish the presence of the Divine Name in tetragrammaton form in that Greek version, it was asserted that this tetragrammaton *must* also have been present in the autographa of the Christian Greek Scriptures.

Afterwards were presented certain Hebrew translations of the New Testament and the manner in which NWT used them to support the *restoration* of the Divine Name to the pages of the Christian Greek Scriptures and, of course, to the pages of the English translation.

How to pronounce the Divine Name formed the next major division. Within this section was discussed the evidence existing for and against the presence of the tetragrammaton in the LXX, and it was concluded that even with evidence pro and con the whole matter was of no real signification. *There exists for NWT a missing link—manuscript evidence—showing that* *the apostles actually used the Divine Name as alleged.* Also, prohibitions concerning the use of God's name and the impasse regarding the vocalization of the name were presented.

The final division presented the heart of the whole matter: the Jesus/Jehovah identification. By means of several tables it was shown by the writer that NWT employed its principle for restoring the name in an inconsistent fashion. Finally, three passages were discussed exegetically and shown objectively and textually to make certain the identification between Jesus and Jehovah.

Thus it has been the desire of the investigator to demonstrate that the greatest single peculiarity of NWT—the ''restoration'' of Jehovah—is based not upon a foundation of ''gold, silver and precious stones,'' but upon that of ''wood, hay and stubble.''

Chapter 4

TRANSLATION OF ΘΕΟΣ
IN *NEW WORLD TRANSLATION*

As the preceding chapter treated of one small part of the entire New Testament, the Divine Name, and while at the same time the implications and importance of something so apparently small were seen to be far-reaching indeed, the present chapter proposes to treat another apparently small part: the translation of the Greek word θεός. There is no issue taken with NWT regarding the *meaning* of this word, for seldom does it mean anything other than "God." The issue arises at first glance out of the arthrous or anarthrous status of the word. *Arthrous* means having "the" before a noun; *anarthrous* is without "the." But the investigator shall endeavor to demonstrate that the issue rises out of a prior "preferred religious view"[1] on the part of the Witnesses and that the arthrous or anarthrous status of θεός became simply a means to a doctrinal end.

Since the position of NWT is stated so precisely in an appendix to John 1:1, the first portion of this chapter will present that appendix and its significations. Next, and stemming from the appendix will follow a discussion of the Greek article. Finally, there will be set forth a listing of θεός as it occurs some 1,305 times and the NWT translation of it.

I. *Appendix to John 1:1—"a god"*

Of all the New Testament passages that may be used to assert Jesus Christ's deity, none other lends itself so readily to the apologist as John 1:1. And if a survey could be taken among Christians who have accosted and have been accosted by Jehovah's Witnesses, this passage would no doubt be seen to have figured prominently in every confrontation. Unfortunately, the Christian layman is more often than not placed immediately on the defensive, because the Witness will invariably launch a Greek-grammar blitzkrieg and "conclusively prove" that Jesus cannot be deity as God is deity.

---

1. New World Translation, p. 6.

The appendix to John 1:1 occupies nearly four pages of NWT. It commences by presenting the rendering of two modern English versions of the verse. *The Complete Bible: An American Translation* renders θεός "divine"—"In the beginning the Word existed. The Word was with God, and the Word was divine." *A New Translation of the Bible* by James Moffatt translates the final clause ". . . The Logos was divine."[2] Immediately following is this statement:

> Every honest person will have to admit that John's saying that the Word or Logos "was divine" is not saying that he was the God with whom he was. It merely tells of a certain quality about the Word or Logos, but it does not identify him as the one and the same as God.[3]

The translation of NWT at John 1:1 bears out this testimony which "every honest person will have to admit." It runs: "Originally the Word was, and the Word was with God, and the Word was a god."[4]

The effect of designating Christ "a god" is at the very least a startling one to the Christian who reads or hears the translation. Certainly, there must be ponderous evidence for such a departure from the almost universal manner in which the verse has been translated in the past—"and the Word was God." NWT is not slow to give the reason, and for clarity it has been deemed best to let the translators speak for themselves explicitly:

> The reason for their rendering the Greek word "divine," and not "God," is that it is the Greek noun *the·os*. The God with whom the Word or Logos was originally is designated here by the Greek expression ὁ θεός *the·os* preceded by the definite article *ho*, hence an articular *the·os*. Careful translators recognize that the articular construction points to a quality about someone.[5]

Hence, to say "divine" is *qualitative;* to say "God" is *quantitative*. In the investigator's opinion the NWT rendering of "a god" is on their basis quantitative, for it is not capitalization of "God" but the presence of the article, we are told, which makes the word quantitative. *Therefore, NWT has not consistently employed this principle even at the outset.*

The appendix continues by quoting the grammarians Dana and Mantey on

---

2. Ibid., p. 773.
3. Ibid.
4. Ibid., p. 282.
5. Ibid., p. 774.

the significance of the article with a predicate nominative. An analogous passage to John 1:1 from Xenophon's *Anabasis* is given, reading: "and the place was a market." The grammarians conclude:

> The article points out the subject in these examples. Neither was *the place* the only market, nor was *the word* all of God, as it would mean if the article were also used with θεός.[6]

The investigator must note that *NWT omitted the last sentence of Dana and Mantey's statement, for reasons most obvious:* "As it stands, the other persons of the Trinity may be implied in θεός."[7] NWT then lightly chides this grammar for not translating θεός "a god" to parallel "a market" in the *Anabasis*.

In order to counter the assertion that has been made by some scholars in the past—that an article before θεός is to be assumed—NWT asseverates:

> . . . it is presumptuous to say that such a definite article is to be understood so that the sentence should therefore be translated "and the Word was God."[8]

Such, they continue, would mean that the Logos is the God with whom he is said to be. "This is unreasonable."[9] Furthermore, it is said, the inspired writings of John and his fellow disciples indicate what the true idea is, namely, that the Logos "is not God or *the* God, but is the Son of God, and hence is a god."[10] Again Dana and Mantey are cited, this time referring to A. T. Robertson, who, in discussing θεός with the article, says that it is treated like a proper name and hence may or may not have it. Dana and Mantey state that they construe him to mean that there is not a definite rule which governs the use of the article with θεός, resulting in difficulty for the reader trying to detect the writer's meaning. Thus NWT:

> The above disposes of the trinitarian argument that the article was omitted before θεός in the predicate of John 1:1 according to the general rule that it was not needed, but would be understood.[11]

---

6. Ibid.
7. H. E. Dana and J. R. Mantey, *A Manual Grammar of the Greek New Testament*, p. 149.
8. *New World Translation*.
9. Ibid.
10. Ibid., p. 775.
11. Ibid., p. 776.

Perhaps the Witnesses expect the Christian church to be comforted over the dispatch with which the doctrine of the Trinity, apparently foisted upon the Scriptures, has been scuttled. "Especially so, since all the doctrine of the sacred Scriptures bears out the correctness of this rendering [a god]."[12]

The remainder of the appendix calls attention to a number of passages in the Gospel of John where the "definite article"[13] precedes the noun in the predicate; and finally, a confession that NWT cannot lay claim to being the first to translate John 1:1 with "a god." The claim must reside with *"The New Testament, in an Improved Version, upon the Basis of Archbishop Newcome's New Translation: with a Corrected Text,* printed in London, 1808."[14]

Such is the contention of NWT in this appendix: straightforward and dogmatic. The writer has sought to present their position through paraphrase and quotation in the same spirit in which it is set forth in their appendix, and he has refrained from inserting personal comment except where deemed necessary.

Significance of This Rendering

What, then, is the import of translating θεός "a god"? If it is simply a matter of the presence or absence of the article, then why cannot a principle be established and followed throughout the New Testament that ὁ θεός be translated "God" and θεός be rendered "a god"? *This is,* to be sure, *the implication of the line of reasoning set forth in the NWT appendix.*

But the trenchant significance of this rendering is that Jesus Christ is not "very God of very God" and the Second Person of the Trinity, but, moreover, He is merely "a god" in a pantheon of lesser divinities. One need only reason with the Witnesses in the following fashion to make this clear: How many Gods are there? There is but one true God, Jehovah God, comes the reply. Is Jesus Christ this God? No, He is "a god," the only begotten Son of Jehovah. Then Jesus Christ must be a "false" god and certainly not to be the recipient of one's worship. No and yes, comes the answer. Jesus in His

---

12. Ibid.

13. Such wording implies the existence of an "indefinite article"; and such an implication reflects lack of understanding of this aspect of the Greek language, for there is no simple parallel in Greek analogous to the English "a" or "an."

14. Ibid., p. 777.

pre-human state was an angel, identified in the Old Testament with Michael and as such God's chief executive officer; [15] therefore, He, like other angels, is not to be worshiped. However, He is unique and worthy of obeisance. [16]

It is not the purpose at this time to take up the implications of Christ as "a god" upon the theology of the New Testament. It is only necessary to enunciate the significance of such a rendering and the problem of polytheism engendered thereby.

II. *The Greek Article*

That the NWT has put great emphasis upon the arthrous or anarthrous state of θεός in John 1:1 is manifested by both the translation of John 1:1 and the appendix to the verse. The Witnesses have stated their position candidly. Now it is incumbent upon the present investigator to examine their "articular" contentions. This section will treat first of the article in classical and Hellenistic[17] usage. Of necessity, this treatment will be quite limited in its scope. The desideratum is to set forth an adequate background for viewing the NWT approach to the article. Second, a definite rule for the use of the article as formulated by E. C. Colwell will be presented.

Classical and Hellenistic Usage

In his doctoral dissertation the reviser of the Blass-Debrunner Greek grammar, Robert W. Funk, presents a recent analysis of the Greek article in both classical and Hellenistic times. [18] The investigator has relied heavily upon his analysis for these Greek periods.

By way of general comment Funk notes that there are several factors which make the article an important element in any stylistic or grammatical study. One is its high frequency. Its constant, and sometimes almost automatic, repetition tends to make it more idiomatic and more revealing of a writer's temperament and disposition; in this respect it compares closely with particles, although exceeding them, of course, in frequency.

Also, the article is characterized by its being a luxury of the language, but

---

15. *The Truth Shall Make You Free*, p. 44, and *New Heavens and a New Earth*, pp. 28-30.

16. It is instructive to observe προσκυνέω in NWT and how the English rendering varies as the word refers to Jehovah God, to Jesus, and to others.

17. The term "Hellenistic" is according to current usage synonymous with Koine.

18. Robert W. Funk, *The Syntax of the Greek Article: Its Importance for Critical Pauline Problems*.

never without meaning. *The Greek article is not necessary for a substantive to be definite;* yet, when the article is used, definiteness is assured and a nuance is added which is not available to authors under different grammatical systems (e.g., Latin).[19]

The article is *deictic* in that it points to something as does an index finger. Thus is apparent the development of the ὁριστικὸν ἄρθρον, as the Greeks called it—"the defining article"—from the demonstrative. But unlike the demonstrative, it does not denote location in space and time. In view of this, Winer states:

> When ὁ, ἡ, τό is employed as strictly an Article before a noun, it marks the object as one definitely conceived, whether in consequence of its nature, or the context, or some circle of ideas assumed as known.[20]

Because the article is deictic, its function is twofold: (1) individual—in that the known, specific, previously recognized individual person or thing is denoted; and (2) generic—in that it refers to class or genus of persons or things.[21]

Grammarians past and present realize the difficulty in making hard and fast rules governing the use of the article. They further agree to the flexibility of this part of speech. Walter Bauer, the outstanding lexicographer, carefully asserts that "gerade hier das Stilgefühl der Schreibenden besonders weiten Spielraum hatte."[22] Funk is very insistent, however, that in the New Testament, as elsewhere, the article is not used without purpose, but that it often depends at the same time on a fineness, an individualistic idiom or a particular nuance for its motive.[23]

In support of this latter statement Winer says:

> In some few instances the use or omission of the article is also a mark of the distinctive style of the writer. Thus Gerstorf has shown . . . that the four evangelists almost always write ὁ χριστός—the expected

---

19. Ibid., p. 3.

20. George B. Winer, *A Grammar of the Idiom of the New Testament,* p. 105.

21. Albert Debrunner, *Friedrich Blass' Grammatik des neutestamentlichen Griechisch,* p. 33, cited by Robert W. Funk, *The Syntax of the Greek Article,* p. 145.

22. Walter Bauer, *Griechisch-Deutsches Wörterbuch zu den Schriften des neuen Testaments und der ubrigen urchristen Literatur,* p. 997, cited by Funk, *The Syntax of the Greek Article,* p. 7. ["exactly here the feeling for style of the writer has especially wide room for play."]

23. Funk, *The Syntax of the Greek Article,* p. 7.

Messiah, like ὁ ἐρχόμενος—while Paul and Peter write χριστός, when this appellation had become more of a proper name.[24]

The noted classical authority Gildersleeve, regarding the variation of articular usage, wrote:

> Dialects vary, and the Doric is said to have affected the hearty homely article. . . . authors vary, and whereas some eschew the article with proper names or use it gingerly, others, like Plato, are exceedingly free with it. On the other hand, the familiar use of the article has led to exactness and finesse, and the subtle variations in the employment of it add a special charm to Attic prose.[25]

In view of these forgone comments one must conclude that the Greek article can be understood and appreciated only through diligent study of it over a long period of time. One must attempt to capture it, as Bauer put it, "das Stilgefühl" of the writer.

In order to aid one in attaining this aim, there are some general observations that may serve as guidelines. The student of Greek must apply these—and others—for himself and prove their validity or invalidity. Since this chapter concerns itself with the translation of θεός these observations are primarily relative to proper names.

Blass-Debrunner, basing comment upon an exhaustive study by Bernhard Weiss,[26] observed that whenever the Jewish or Christian God is in view, the article is present, but that it may be omitted after prepositions and if in the genitive when depending on an anarthrous noun.[27] Funk states that it is not generally agreed that the use of the article with θεός does not depend upon the syntax, but upon the term's essential meaning in each context. He admits this to be perhaps too much of an overstatement of the actual situation because some grammarians would modify this "rule" considerably. As early as Green, he notes, the article was recognized to be a tool for denoting nuances of meaning. And Green held that θεός and ὁ θεός are used almost interchangeably, but acknowledged that the anarthrous noun lays stress on

---

24. George B. Winer, *A Treatise on the Grammar of New Testament Greek,* cited by Funk, cited in ibid.

25. Basil L. Gildersleeve, *A Syntax of Classical Greek,* Part II, p. 514, cited by Funk, *The Syntax of the Greek Article,* p. 4.

26. Berhard Weiss, "Der Gebrauch des Artikels bei den Gottesnamen," *Theologische Studien und Kritiken,* pp. 319-92, 503-38.

27. Debrunner, *Friedrich Blass' Grammatik,* p. 251,1.

the divine character while the arthrous specifies the Christian God.[28]

From Plato to Paul the Greek article has appeared as an integral and viable part of the language. In the Papyri and in Patristics it continued to retain its vitality. It defies being constricted by narrow grammatical rules, but it also defies the charge of ambiguity. And it is with all this in mind that one must view the translation by NWT of John 1:1 and their definitive principle by which this rendering is defended: ὁ θεός is "God" and θεός is "a god."

The NWT appendix to John 1:1 carefully demonstrates that "the articular construction of the noun points to an identity, a personality, whereas an anarthrous construction points to a quality about someone."[29] The simplicity and usefulness of this "rule" would be welcomed, no doubt by all scholars. However, the discussion of the matter in the preceding section on the article in classical and Hellenistic usage nullifies the NWT attempt at so great simplification.

In 1933 an endeavor was made to delineate a definite rule[30] for the use of the article in the Greek New Testament. Ernest C. Colwell—then of the University of Chicago—outlined his discovery in the *Journal of Biblical Literature* entitled "A Definite Rule for the Use of the Article in the Greek New Testament."[31]

Colwell's conclusion may be summed up in one definitive paragraph. Referring to John 1:49; 5:27; and 9:5, he says:

> It was a study of these passages, especially John 1:49, that suggested the rule which is advocated in this study. In the verse Nathanael ascribes to Jesus two titles; in one of them he uses the article, in the other he does not: σὺ εἶ ὁ υἱὸς τοῦ θεοῦ· σὺ βασιλεὺς εἶ τοῦ Ἰσραήλ. What reason is there for this difference? When the passage is scrutinized, it appears at once that the variable quantum is not the definiteness but word-order. "King of Israel" in this context is as definite as "Son of God." It seems probable that the article is used with "Son of God" because it follows the verb, and is not used with "King of Israel" because it preceded the verb. If this can be established generally in the New Testament, it will of course involve only those sentences in which the copula is expressed. And for such sentences the rule may be stated briefly as follows: A

---

28. Funk, *The Syntax of the Greek Article*, p. 144.
29. *New World Translation*, p. 774.
30. Abbreviated by the present investigator as "Colrule."
31. E. C. Colwell, "A Definite Rule for the Use of the Article in the Greek New Testament," *Journal of Biblical Literature* LII (1933), pp. 12-21.

definite predicate nominative has the article when it follows the verb; it does not have the article when it precedes the verb. Of course, this can be claimed as a rule only after it has been shown to describe the usage of the Greek New Testament as a whole or in large part.[32]

The proposed rule, then, is thus: *A definite predicate nominative has the article when it follows the verb; it does not have the article when it precedes the verb.*

Examples supporting the rule from the New Testament. John 19:21 illustrates Colrule aptly. "King of the Jews" arthrously and anarthrously refers to Jesus: Μὴ γράφε ὁ βασιλεὺς τῶν Ἰουδαίων, ἀλλ᾽ ὅτι ἐκεῖνος εἶπεν βασιλεὺς τῶν Ἰουδαίων εἰμί. The Jews objected to the superscription in that it may be read as a factual statement and wished to have it changed to a claim made by Jesus. Either way the definiteness of "King" remains the same, but in the second instance the word is anarthrous, and thus, it would seem, *because it preceded* the verb. In these passages—Matthew 27:11, 37; Mark 15:2; Luke 23:3, 37; and John 18:33—King of the Jews appears with the article *after the verb*. In Matthew 27:42 the same title is anarthrous and before the verb.[33]

Two other supporting examples, also titles, are "Son of God" and "Son of Man." Son of God appears about eleven times arthrously as a predicate and following the verb.[34] Ten times it anarthrously appears as predicate. Of these, nine precede the verb.[35] The apparent exception is Matthew 27:43, where θεοῦ interestingly precedes the verb. The title Son of Man appears twice as a predicate nominative. Matthew 13:37 is arthrous and follows the verb. In John 5:27 it is anarthrous and precedes the verb.[36]

Frequently the same phrase in the same Gospel varies only with regard to the article and word order. For example, in John 8:12 Jesus says, Ἐγώ εἰμι τὸ φῶς τοῦ κόσμου; in 9:5, φῶς εἰμὶ τοῦ κόσμου. Similarly, in Matthew 12:48 and 50 Jesus uses "my mother" arthrously after the verb and anarthrously before the verb.[37]

---

32. Ibid., p. 13.
33. Ibid.
34. Matt. 16:16; 26:63; Mark 3:11; Luke 4:41; 22:70; John 1:49; 11:27; 20:31; Acts 9:20; I John 4:15; 5:5.
35. Matt. 4:3, 6; 14:33; 27:40, 54; Mark 15:39; Luke 4:3, 9; John 10:36.
36. Colwell, *A Definite Rule*, p. 14.
37. Ibid.

The Matthean account of the explanation of the parable of the sower, 13:37-39, impressively supports Colrule. The passage contains a series of seven clauses with seven predicate nouns. The initial five are articular and follow the verb, while the last two, equally definite, are anarthrous and *precede* the verb. The clauses run:

1. ὁ σπείρων τὸ καλὸν σπέρμα ἐστὶν ὁ υἱὸς τοῦ ἀνθρώπου·
2. ὁ δὲ ἀγρός ἐστιν ὁ κόσμος·
3. τὸ δὲ καλὸν σπέρμα, οὗτοί εἰσιν οἱ υἱοὶ τῆς βασιλείας·
4. τὰ δὲ ζιζάνιά εἰσιν οἱ υἱοὶ τοῦ πονηροῦ,
5. ὁ δὲ ἐχθρὸς ὁ σπείρας αὐτά ἐστιν ὁ διάβολος·
6. ὁ δὲ θερισμὸς συντέλεια αἰῶνός ἐστιν,
7. οἱ δὲ θερισταὶ ἄγγελοί εἰσιν.

Ostensibly, Matthew altered the order of words for variety of style, but he maintained definiteness for the predicate nouns by omitting the article and placing them before the verb. Matthew 23:8-10 furnishes an analogous passage. And in neither can it be claimed that the anarthrous predicates are any less definite or concrete than the arthrous.[38]

Colwell points out that the grammarians Robertson and Blass-Debrunner list in their grammars predicates having the article and not having the article which almost without exception fall into the categories established by Colrule. "No one," he states, will be so unkind as to insinuate that these lists were compiled to support a theory of which the compilers had never heard."[39]

Further support, Colwell cites, reveals itself in variant readings of New Testament manuscripts. Three such variants are as follows:

(1) John 1:49

B (Vaticanus)
σὺ βασιλεὺς εἶ τοῦ Ἰσραήλ

א (Sinaiticus)
σὺ εἶ ὁ βασιλεὺς τοῦ Ἰσραήλ

(2) Matthew 23:10

καθηγητὴς ὑμῶν ἐστιν εἷς   εἷς γὰρ ὑμῶν ἐστιν ὁ καθηγητής

(3) James 2:19

εἷς θεός ἐστιν   εἷς ἐστιν ὁ θεός

---

38. Ibid.
39. Ibid., p. 15.

Interestingly, B each time places the anarthrous predicate before the verb and ℵ each time puts the articular predicate after the verb. Ostensibly, the scribes felt that a definite predicate noun before the verb did not need the article but did need it after the verb.[40]

Other support from the New Testament itself can be furnished, and Colwell does supply it in his study. Only that has been presented here which the investigator deemed minimal for establishing the plausibility of Colrule.

Examples supporting the rule from outside the New Testament. Although based upon a hurried sampling of Greek usage outside the New Testament, Colwell asserts that the results generally support his findings in the New Testament. In Genesis, chapters 1–41, he counted some fifty-eight definite predicate nouns. Of these, forty-five support Colrule—for example, 4:20 and 12:12; thirteen are exceptions, as 9:18. He also notes that the same kind of manuscript variation exists in 9:19 as in the New Testament. Codex Alexandrinus contains the arthrous predicate after the verb, while Cotton Genesis manuscript reads it anarthrously before the verb. Other samplings come from the Didache, Papyrus Oxyrhynchus III, and the *Discourses* of Epictetus IV.[41]

Exceptions to the rule. In the New Testament these number about fifteen that vary from the rule that a definite predicate noun is anarthrous before the verb.[42] Half are scattered through Luke, John, II Peter, and Revelation. In five of these there is significant manuscript evidence for omitting the article in compliance with Colrule. The other half of these exceptions occur in the Corinthian letters. Of these seven, five place the predicate noun not only before the verb but before the subject as well: for example, I Corinthians 9:1 reads οὐ τὸ ἔργον μου ὑμεῖς ἐστε ἐν κυρίῳ; Colwell suggests that this is "a stylism temporarily affected by the apostle to the Gentiles, possibly for the sake of greater emphasis."[43]

That class of exceptions which omits the article after the verb contains more examples—approximately twenty-six.[44] Since proper names regularly

40. Ibid., p. 6.
41. Ibid., p. 19.
42. Luke 4:41; John 1:21; 6:51; 15:1; II Pet. 1:17; Rom. 4:13; I Cor. 9:1, 2; 11:3, 25; II Cor. 1:12; 3:2, 17; Rev. 19:8; 20:14.
43. Ibid., p. 18.
44. Matt. 20:16; Mark 4:32; 9:35; 12:28; Luke 20:33; 22:24; John 4:18; 18:13, 37; Acts 10:36; Rom. 4:11, 18; 7:13; 8:16, 29; 11:6; I Cor. 12:27; 16:25; II Cor. 5:21; 6:16; Gal. 4:31; I Thess. 4:3; I Pet. 5:12; Heb. 11:1.

omit the article in the predicate when following the verb, they are not included as exceptions. Two of the exceptions are quotations from the LXX; five are substantivized adjectives. The rest have no common characteristics. Two—I Corinthians 12:27 and I Thessalonians 4:3—have textual evidence giving some basis for reading in accordance with Colrule. The most notable feature in this list is the large number of exceptions in Romans.[45]

Importance of Colrule. This rule has vital implications in at least three fields of New Testament study: grammar, text, and translation or interpretation. Future grammars will no longer merely say that predicate nouns regularly omit the article. They must say that, when the copula occurs, about two-thirds of the definite predicate nouns *do* have the article. Colwell's work renders such a general statement as too vague. Instead the following rules may be formulated tentatively:

> (1) Definite predicate nouns here regularly take the article. (2) The exceptions are for the most part due to a change in word-order: (a) Definite predicate nouns which follow the verb (this is the usual order) usually take the article; (b) Definite predicate nouns which precede the verb usually lack the article; (c) Proper names regularly lack the article in the predicate; (d) Predicate nominatives in relative clauses regularly follow the verb whether or not they have the article.[46]

In the field of textual criticism Colrule makes an equally definite contribution. "It shows in certain specific cases what the probabilities are as to the author's use or non-use of the article."[47] II Peter 1:17 is a good example. Westcott and Hort, following, of course, Vaticanus, read ὁ υἱός μου ὁ ἀγαπητός μου οὗτός ἐστιν. Since the evidence set forth in Colwell's study points to the extreme rarity of this type construction in the New Testament, Tischendorf's judgment that the more greatly attested reading is οὗτός ἐστιν ὁ υἱός μου ὁ ἀγαπητός μου, is to be preferred.

The areas of translation and interpretation receive the greatest light from this rule. *No longer can a predicate noun preceding the verb be translated as indefinite or qualitatively solely because no article is present.* If the context reveals that the predicate is definite, then it ought to be translated as a definite noun despite the absence of the article. *Contrariwise, when a*

---

45. Ibid., pp. 18-19.
46. Ibid., p. 20.
47. Ibid.

predicate noun is anarthrous following the verb, the probability that it is indefinite is very great. In summary Colwell remarks:

> Loosely speaking, this study may be said to have increased the definiteness of a predicate noun before the verb without the article, and to have decreased the definiteness of a predicate noun after the verb without the article.[48]

In his concluding comments he cites John 1:1 as one of the many verses where this rule suggests translating an anarthrous predicate as definite. "Καὶ θεὸς ἦν ὁ λόγος looks much more like 'And the Word was God' than 'And the Word was divine' when viewed with reference to this rule."[49] As has been previously emphasized, such an anarthrous predicate noun is indefinite in this position *only if demanded by the context.*

> The context makes no such demand in the Gospel of John, for this statement cannot be regarded as strange in the prologue of the gospel which reaches its climax in the confession of Thomas.[50]

The present investigator strongly inclines toward the results of Colwell's study and believes that serious grammatical and theological criticism must treat of this rule, either furthering its verification or completely demolishing it. More than four decades have passed since Colwell set forth his view. To the knowledge of this writer, no exhaustive investigation has yet transpired during this time. However, his work has not passed unnoticed.

Bruce Metzger, writing in *Theology Today* in 1953, and discussing the Jehovah's Witnesses, refers to NWT of John 1:1 and quotes a paragraph from Colwell's article which defines Colrule. Metzger states that NWT, in translating "and the Word was a god," overlooked entirely "an established rule of Greek grammar which necessitates the rendering, '. . . and the Word was God.' "[51] Ten years later the author of the third volume of Moulton's work on Greek grammar, Nigel Turner, makes mention of Colrule:

> In Colwell's count, which is somewhat arbitrary, only 15 articular

48. Ibid., p. 21.

49. Ibid.

50. Ibid. For Thomas's confession see John 20:28, where Jesus is designated ὁ κυριός μου καὶ ὁ θεός μου.

51. Bruce M. Metzger, "The Jehovah's Witnesses and Jesus Christ," *Theology Today*, pp. 65-85.

predicate nouns precede the verb, while 239 follow it, and only 40 anarthrous predicate nouns follow the verb while 99 precede it. Judicious selection among the MS variants may remove some of the exceptions to Colwell's canon but cannot remove all. So that while the canon may reflect a general tendency it is not absolute by any means; after all, it takes no account of relative clauses or proper nouns, and he has also omitted a considerable class of "qualitative" nouns like that in ὁ θεὸς ἀγάπη ἐστιν. Moreover, he is the first to admit the lack of objectivity in his method of counting: he professes to include only *definite* nouns among his anarthrous predicates, and the degree of definiteness is extremely difficult to assess.[52]

Although Turner's remarks are somewhat pessimistic, he does admit that the rule "may reflect a general tendency." Colrule does not admit to being absolute; nor does a host of other Greek grammatical rules. The last word regarding Colrule remains to be uttered, and may never be; but the first word demands a confrontation with anarthrous nouns which may very well be very definite.

Students of NT Greek ought to speak of the *presence* or *absence* of the *article* rather than that a noun *lacks* the article. "Lack" implies that it *ought* to be there, thus obscuring a nuance of Greek.

Table of ΘΕΟΣ as Translated in NWT

Having received impetus from NWT's appendix to John 1:1, which attempted to justify "a god" for θεός, the investigator observed every occurrence of ὁ θεός, θεός in the New Testament. The number of occurrences exceeds 1300. The standard work chosen for the survey was Moulton and Geden's *Concordance to the Greek Testament;* and each entry was checked against the Nestle text—and that of Westcott and Hort where a variant regarding the article exists. In the table on page 105 each occurrence of θεός is noted by book, chapter, and verse, whether arthrous or anarthrous, and NWT rendering of it. The purpose is clear and simple. The reader may observe the consistency or inconsistency with which NWT has followed the principle enunciated in the John 1:1 appendix.

In the New Testament there are 282 occurrences of the anarthrous θεός. At sixteen places NWT has either a god, god, gods, or godly. Sixteen out of

---

52. Nigel Turner, *Syntax* (vol. III of *A Grammar of New Testament Greek,* ed. James H. Moulton), p. 184.

282 means that the translators were faithful to *their* translation principle only six percent of the time. *To be ninety-four percent unfaithful hardly commends a translation to careful readers!*

The table, having spoken for itself, punctuates the arbitrary manner with which the translators of NWT have handled the sacred text. If one is not justified in demanding that they render every anarthrous θεός "a god," surely one is justified in demanding that the same be translated *qualitatively,* perhaps "divine"—neither of which was done.

The first section of John—1:1-18—furnishes a lucid example of NWT arbitrary dogmatism. Θεός occurs eight times—verses 1, 2, 6, 12, 13, 18—and has the article only twice—verses 1, 2. Yet NWT six times translated "God," once "a god," and once "the god." In the latter instance NWT uses "the" *where there is no article expressed in the Greek text!*

Other examples are numerous which show this arbitrary manipulation of the article with words other than θεός. For example, in Luke 11:24 NWT reads, "When an unclean spirit comes out of a man . . ." where the Greek text reads *"the* unclean spirit" and *"the* man." On the other hand verse 27 in NWT, "and the breasts that you sucked," interpolates an article before "breasts" where there is none in the Greek. Similarly, in James 1:25, "he who peers into the perfect law," one finds no article before "law" in the original. Examples like these could be multiplied at great length.

Conclusion

The writer has not endeavored in this chapter to offer an interpretation for the translation of "And the Word was God." Instead he has attempted to set forth the position of NWT and examine it for validity and consistency.

The NWT appendix explaining the rendering of John 1:1 was set forth in order to observe precisely what prompted this rendering. The basis for "a god," it was seen, is the anarthrous status of θεός. This translation was alleged to have been elicited purely on the basis of grammatical and not religious motivations. The significance of this rendition was pointed out by the investigator to be (1) the formulation of a simple principle of grammar—ὁ θεός="God" and θεός="a god"; and (2) that Christianity is polytheistic—Jesus Christ is a god, and a good god, but not "very God of very God."

For viewing the NWT treatment of θεός in the broad background of classical and Hellenistic Greek, there was discussed briefly the use of the Greek article in those two periods. The general consensus of opinion based upon observation of usage was that the article is part of the genius of language and does not admit of hard and fast rules. But it was pointed out that the article is by no means an ambiguous item. Rather it must be appreciated and felt than learned.

Following this section appeared that which proposed to build upon preceding grammatical studies: Colwell's Rule. Here is an attempt to go beyond the general but at the same time to remain within that sphere. Colrule suggests that anarthrous predicate nouns preceding the expressed copula may be regarded as definite if the context so implies. That this rule may prove very valuable was seen by Colwell's application of it to grammar, text, and interpretation. And with regard to the latter he emphasized the traditional translation, ''And the Word was God.'' In support of Colrule, examples from the New Testament, the LXX, and non-biblical literature were presented. Exceptions to the rule were noted, having been observed by Colwell himself, to aid in securing the validity of the rule.

Finally, and most importantly, table V demonstrated how NWT applied or did not apply its principle formulated in the appendix to John 1:1. *And it is the investigator's firm conclusion that NWT demonstrates utter disregard for the canon thus set forth in its own appendix.* This is not to obviate the element of correctness which certainly exists in the canon, because an anarthrous noun may very well be qualitative and vice versa. But the arbitrary way in which the canon is laid down with reference to John 1:1 and not throughout the New Testament is totally unacceptable to serious scholarship. It bears repeating: NWT has been 94 percent of the time unfaithful to its own principle of translation.

This chapter has undertaken a discussion of the translation, ''And the Word was God''; the next shall discuss *why* the New Testament writers believed the Word *is* God.

Chapter 5

EXCISION OF THE DEITY OF CHRIST
AND THE HOLY SPIRIT THROUGH TRANSLATION

The preceding chapter concerned itself with the translation of καὶ θεὸς ἦν ὁ λόγος. The present will concern itself with *why* the Word *is* God and not merely "a god" or simply "divine." Tangent to Christ's deity is the deity and personality of the Holy Spirit. The subjects of this chapter are inseparable from the Christian concept of God, for it is the triune God that must command the attention of all serious, investigative scholarship and not some alleged, abstract principle of deity or "ground of being."[1] Most Christians believe the Scriptures teach that:

> There be three persons in the Godhead, the Father, the Son, and the Holy Ghost; and these three are one true, eternal God, the same in substance, equal in power and glory; although distinguished by their personal properties.[2]

The present investigator affirms this pivotal doctrine of Christianity and hopes in some small way further to establish it with the consideration of the several passages in this chapter drawn from the New Testament.

Several passages have been selected for their trenchant relevance to the deity of Christ and of the Holy Spirit. These will be examined in the NWT to show if there has been excision, by way of translating, of deity. Careful attention to the Greek text and to the *analogia Scriptura* will be given. The material will be subsumed under Christ and the Holy Spirit.

I. *The Deity of Christ*

John 1:1

That this passage most lucidly and emphatically asseverates Christ's deity, if the Greek text is allowed to read, "And the Word was God," cannot

---

1. Paul Tillich, *The Courage to Be,* pp. 156-60, 172, 180-81. See also his *Systematic Theology*, vol. I, pt. 2, "Being and God," pp. 162-286.

2. *The Confession of Faith, the Larger Catechism,* p. 52.

be controverted. And that NWT's "and the Word was a god" must inevitably imply a type of polytheism also cannot be controverted.

The preceding chapter demonstrated that the absence of the article with "God" does not inviolably render the word qualitative. NWT denominates the anarthrous θεός qualitative, "divine," and then proceeds to translate it quantitatively: "a god." Even if θεός were admitted to be qualitative, one must ask if the apostle meant "divine" (1) as the Caesars were regarded to be divine; or (2) as Satan is divine in that he is "the god of this world";[3] or (3) as God Himself is divine; or (4) as qualified by some other category of divinity which the Witnesses have discovered and apply only to Jesus Christ.

The present investigator, swayed by the overall tenor of John's Gospel, cannot refrain from concurring with Colwell when he says that "And the Word was God" may not be regarded strange in a Gospel that concludes with Thomas' exclamation, "My Lord, and my God!" Even the thoroughgoing destructive criticism of Rudolph Bultmann, though placing John's Gospel in the late second century, would admit that "John" held a very high view of Christ's uniqueness and regarded the Word to be God. Hence, the tenor of John must be admitted to support the translation, "And the Word was God."

In support of NWT's assertion that θεός is *qualitative* are the two New Testament scholars Alford and Westcott. The former says concerning John 1:1:

> Θεός must then be taken as implying God, *in substance,*—not ὁ θεός, "the Father," *in Person*. It does not equal θεῖος nor is it to be rendered *a God*.[4]

And the latter states:

> The predicate (God) stands emphatically first, as in iv. 24. It is necessarily without the article (θεός not ὁ θεός) inasmuch as it describes the nature of the Word and does not identify His Person.[5]

The qualitative character of θεός, they show, in no way diminishes Christ's deity but rather explicates it. Therefore, whether explaining John 1:1 on the basis of Colrule or as do Alford, Westcott, and others, this deity is retained

---

3. II Cor. 4:4.
4. Henry Alford, *The Greek Testament*, vol. I, p. 681.
5. B. F. Westcott, *The Gospel According to St. John*, p. 3.

and not exscinded as in NWT, "and the Word was a god."

John 20:28

In this passage containing Thomas' ejaculation of faith, NWT reads, "My Master and My God!" The Greek is ὁ κυριός μου καὶ ὁ θεός μου, and ὁ θεός *must* refer to Jesus. The parallelism is too great to allow "Lord" or "Master" to refer to Jesus and "God" to Jehovah. No charge of excision can be made here against NWT; however, there is in evidence *a strange silence* in a book where footnotes abound.

Acts 20:28

Truly a difficult verse to translate because of both textual and theological considerations, this translation of it is found in NWT:

> Pay attention to yourselves and to all the flock, among which the holy spirit has appointed YOU overseers, to shepherd the congregation of God, which he purchased with the blood of his own [Son].

To this verse is appended a footnote directing the reader to the Appendix, where there is a discussion of Acts 20:28.

Two problems confront the translator: (1) whether to read τὴν ἐκκλησίαν τοῦ θεοῦ or τὴν ἐκκλησίαν τοῦ κυρίου; and (2) whether to translate "with the blood of his own [Son]" or "with his own blood." These must be studied both individually and together. As touching the first, one notices the speaker here to be the Apostle Paul. His epistles contain eleven instances of the phrase, "the church of God" and none to "the church of the Lord." Hence, at the outset Pauline usage favors reading "the church of God." However, to read "the church of God which he purchased with his own blood" immediately poses a difficult thought: How can it be said that God gave His blood for His church? For those ancient and modern men who deny the Incarnation, this certainly is in the realm of the inconceivable.

The second part of the matter is more related to translation than to the textual reading, for no variant exists which reads "Son" after "his own." The possibilities for translation are (1) "the church of the Lord which he purchased with his own blood"; (2) "the church of God which he purchased with the blood of his own [Son]"; or (3) "the church of God which he purchased with his own blood."

NWT has chosen (2) for the following reasons. First, even though manuscripts P74 ACD Harkleian Syriac (margin) and others read "the church of the Lord," NWT follows the text supported by B ℵ Vulgate and others. The external evidence is certainly not decisive, but—having established their text primarily upon Westcott and Hort—the balance sways toward the reading, "the church of God." However, ℵ BVg "read 'God' (articulate), and the ordinary translation would mean to say 'God's blood' "[6] And this is the second reason for NWT's rendering "with the blood of his own [Son]." The Appendix to this verse states that the two troublesome Greek words are τοῦ ἰδίου, "his own," following the phrase "with the blood." It is readily seen, continues the Appendix, that the entire expression could be rendered "with the blood of his own." Therefore:

> A noun in the singular number would be understood after "his own," most likely God's closest relative, his only-begotten Son Jesus Christ.[7]

Building upon this, NWT apparently agrees with G. C. Knapp's textual emendation that "Son" was originally a part of the Greek text—τοῦ ἰδίου υἰοῦ. Weymouth's footnote in his New Testament is quoted, noting that if such were the original text it is easily seen how υἰοῦ, all but identical to ἰδίου, could have been accidentally omitted. NWT concludes by saying:

> We have retained the ℵ B reading of the articulate θεοῦ and have rendered the passage literally, adding "Son" in brackets after the ἰδίου to read: "the congregation of God which he purchased with the blood of his own [Son]."[8]

So runs the justification for translating Acts 20:28 in this fashion.

By way of criticism, the present investigator freely admits the difficulty of the passage. In the first place, one ought to observe that NWT, by interpolating "Son" in brackets, has taken a liberty with the text, a liberty eschewed by the translators in the Foreword, a liberty found "interwoven" into other translations "to color the thought."[9] This liberty is further *absolutized* when  one realizes that no extant manuscript contains υἰοῦ after τοῦ ἰδίου. NWT "adds" to the sacred text a word *based solely upon conjecture*. And this

---

6. *New World Translation*, p. 777.
7. Ibid.
8. Ibid., p. 778.
9. Ibid., pp. 6, 9.

addition irrefragably stems from "a preferred religious view,"[10] a Socinian view of Jesus Christ.

In the second place, viewing τοῦ ἰδίου as requiring υἱοῦ after it is without New Testament parallel. Metzger comments on this verse:

> This absolute use of the singular number of ἴδιος, which is otherwise unknown in the New Testament, is found occasionally in the Greek papyri as a term of endearment referring to near relatives.[11]

He further states that it is possible that early Christians gave to Jesus the title ὁ ἴδιος, "his Own," comparable to "the Beloved,"ὁ ἀγαπητός. Paul explicitly asserts in Romans 8:32 that God did not spare τοῦ ἰδίου υἱοῦ.[12]

The more difficult reading is "the church *of God* which he purchased with His own blood." A scribe would have thus been more likely to change "God" to read "Lord" than the reverse. In connection with the Arian controversy which raged over the Person of Christ is Alford's still cogent reasoning:

> If the passage is of such a nature, that, *whichever reading is adopted, the orthodox meaning is legitimate,* but *the adoption of the stronger orthodox reading is absolutely incompatible with the heretical meaning,*—then it is probable that *such stronger orthodox reading was the original.* For while the heretics would be certain to annul the expression offensive to them and substitute the weaker one, the orthodox, on the above hypothesis, would have originally no motive for alteration.[13]

The NWT Appendix lists several New Testament passages from Moulton's *Grammar* which apparently illustrate that a noun should follow τοῦ ἰδίου. The passages are John 1:11; 13:1; and Acts 4:23; 24:23. The investigator, however, sees little analogy between these and the τοῦ ἰδίου of Acts 20:28. Each instance is in the plural and in each context the following noun to be understood, also in the plural, is quite clear. A cursory glance at the occurrences of ὁ ἴδιος in the New Testament reveals that when it is used in the singular its following noun is almost always stated and not left to be understood. The present writer suggests that the more difficult translation be

---

10. Ibid., p. 6.
11. Metzger, *The Text of the New Testament*, p. 236.
12. Ibid.
13. Alford, *Greek Testament*, I, p. 83.

adopted and that διὰ τοῦ αἵματος τοῦ ἰδίου be allowed to say as it literally may, "through His own blood.

Romans 9:5

Long a touchstone for determining the christological tenor of a Bible translation, Romans 9:5 remains such with regard to NWT. Paul commences the chapter with his impassionate concern for the salvation of his Israelite kinsmen who were recipients of the adoption, the Shekinah, the covenants, the law, the divine service, and the promises: (NWT) "to whom the forefathers belong and from whom Christ sprang according to the flesh: God who is over all be blest forever. Amen."[14] To this verse is a footnote directing the reader to see the Appendix under Romans 9:5. Turning to it one notices incidentally that it follows the Appendix of Acts 20:28.

The Greek text under discussion is given: ὁ ὢν ἐπὶ πάντων θεὸς εὐλογητὸς εἰς τοὺς αἰῶνας ἀμήν; and the Greek grammarians Sanday, Headlam, J. H. Moulton, and Robertson are cited to point out that the problem is rather a matter of exegesis and punctuation than grammar. NWT concludes:

> We take the passage as a reference to God and as pronouncing a blessing upon him for the provisions just named which He has made, and have so rendered it: "God who is over all be blest forever. Amen." The grammar of the Greek text admits of this.[15]

Finally, the Appendix lists three versions which agree with NWT: *An American Translation* by Moffatt, *The Riverside New Testament,* and the Revised Standard Version. Since NWT was published, the New English Bible has appeared and agrees also at this point. For what it is worth, some versions disagreeing with NWT are the lineage of the King James, English Revised, and American Standard versions; Luther's German translation, Douay-Rheims; those of Ivan Panin, Charles B. Williams, and Gerrit Verkuyl; the Amplified New Testament, and the Catholic revision of Rheims: the Confraternity edition.

Robertson's complete statement in the Appendix is worthy of note:

---

14. *New World Translation,* p. 471.
15. Ibid., p. 779.

As is well known, the difficulty here is a matter of exegesis and the punctuation of the editor will be made according to his theology. But it may be said in brief that the natural way to take ὁ ὤν and θεὸς is in apposition to ὁ χριστός.[16]

If the reader begins at verse one and reads through to verse five, this investigator believes that the "natural way" will present itself in much the same manner as Robertson describes it. The unnatural way, as rendered by NWT and others, therefore, means that NWT must assume the burden of proof for its justification and demonstrate that it is not excising the deity of Jesus Christ because of theological considerations. This, in the opinion of the writer, cannot be done.

The natural way of reading the verse can be supported by grammar itself, Robertson's statement respectfully notwithstanding, Charles Hodge, in his *Commentary on the Epistle to the Romans,* presents a masterful exegesis of the verse and concludes that grammatically the natural way of translating it is the only way consonant with the context. The words ὁ ὤν are the equivalent of ὅς ἐστι as in the analogous constructions of John 1:18; 12:17; and II Corinthians 11:31. The last passage ought specifically to be observed, since it is (1) Pauline and (2) more analogous to Romans 9:5 than the others.

The words ὁ ἐπὶ πάντων θεός frequently appear in the writings of the Greek fathers as designating the supreme God. Hodge remarks, "It is not the relation of the persons of the Trinity, however, which is here brought into view, but simply the true and supreme divinity of our Lord."[17]

This conclusion is demanded by the context because of the thought antithesis initiated by κατὰ σάρκα. Paul in effect says, "The Messiah, Jesus, on the one hand sprang from Jewish stock, but on the other hand He is of the nature of deity." To designate Jesus as "God over all things" is not inconsonant with the Savior's own words recorded by the evangelist, Matthew 28:18: "To Me was given all authority in heaven and upon the earth."

Hodge, as does Alford, observes the attempt to punctuate the verse so as to make a doxology to God the Father. The classicist Erasmus proposed that a full stop be placed after σάρκα, thus following the punctuation of two twelfth-century cursives, 5 and 47. The objection to this manner of punctuat-

---

16. Ibid.
17. Charles Hodge, *Commentary on the Epistle to the Romans,* p. 300.

ing the verse thus far has never been obviated. None other than Socinius himself suggested this objection. He noted that without exception[18] in either Hebrew or Greek, wherever ascription of blessing is found, the predicate εὐλόγητος or בָּרוּךְ precedes the name of God. So thoroughly convinced is Alford that he asseverates:

> The rendering given above is then not only that most agreeable to the usage of the Apostle, *but the only one admissible by the rules of grammar and arrangement.* It also admirably suits the context: for, having enumerated the historic advantages of the Jewish people, he concludes by stating one which ranks far higher than all,—that from them sprung, according to the flesh, He who is God over all, blessed for ever.[19]

The NWT, by adopting the translation it sets forth, which draws a disjuncture between Jesus Christ and God, goes contrary to the natural way of reading Romans 9:1-5 and contrary to the gravity of the proofs which have been adduced to support it.

Colossians 2:9

To this extremely relevant christological passage NWT has provided no appendix. The translation runs: "because it is in him that all the fullness of the divine quality dwells for the body." A footnote offers also the translation "dwells bodily." In this passage there is no question of grammar, but there is the question of how to translate the Greek word θεότης. Concommitantly, its synonym θειότης in Romans 1:20, both hapaxlegomena, must be treated.

NWT renders θειότης in Romans 1:20 as "Godship." Readily, one realizes that "Godship" is much stronger than "divine quality." But the question must be asked, Is this the thrust that obtains in the words in Greek?

The Authorized Version rendered both Greek words by "Godhead," an unfortunate ambiguity. Though the two are generally in the class of synonyms, "yet they must not be regarded as identical in meaning, nor even as two different forms of the same word," writes the philologist R. C. Trench. He further notes the diverse derivations of the words: θεότης being from

---

18. The one apparent exception is Ps. 67:19-20, where the LXX has εὐλογητός twice, and the first is without parallel in the Hebrew text.

19. Alford, *The Greek Testament*, II, p. 406.

θεός; and θειότης, not from τὸ θεῖον, but from θεῖος, an adjective.[20] In the Latin version, owing to the poverty of that language in this area, both Greek words are rendered by the one Latin word *divinitas*. But that this was wholly inadequate may be seen by the fact that later the word *deitas* was coined to represent θειότης. The German translator De Wette tried to express the distinction obtaining between the words by rendering θειότης by *Göttlichkeit* and θεότης by *Gottheit*.

Both words are abstract and as such are of late introduction. Θεότης is exceedingly a *rara avis*, being logged but three times in extant Greek writings. Thrice it occurs in Plutarch's *Moralia*. The more didactic occurrence is that in his De Def. Orac. 10:

Οὕτως ἐκ μὲν ἀνθρώπων εἰς ἥρωας, ἐκ δὲ ἡρώων εἰς δαίμονας, αἱ βελτίωνες ψυχαὶ τὴν μεταβολὴν λαμβάνουσιν. ἐκ δὲ δαιμόνων ὀλίγαι μὲν ἔτι χρόνῳ πολλῷ δι' ἀρετῆς καθαρθεῖσαι παντάπασι θεότητος μετέσχον.[21]

Trench sees in this passage and the other two agreement with the meaning he is seeking to establish: the Godhead in its absolute sense insofar as "the heathen could conceive it."[22]

Θειότης, much commoner, upholds the distinction set forth by Trench. "There is ever a manifestation of the divine, of some divine attributes, in that to which θειότης is attributed, but never absolute essential Deity," he comments. For example, Lucian designates Hephaestion θειότης in that Alexander posthumously would have raised him to the rank of a god. Plutarch writes of the θειότης τῆς ψυχῆς and uses the word similarly in other passages.[23]

In the Romans context Paul discusses man's "apologetic" bankruptcy, recording that God's Special Revelation enables him to know God's eternality and "divinity," θειότης, and thus renders all men everywhere ἀναπολογήτους (without excuse). Θειότης appears to be a substantivized adjective here, and as "divinity" is here more fitting than the word used in

---

20. Richard C. Trench, *Synonyms of the New Testament*, p. 7.

21. Ibid., p. 10. ["Thus, some of men become Heroes, but others of Heroes become divinities, the better souls receiving the transformation. And of the divinities some few still in much time through virtue are purified completely and partake of *Deity*."]

22. Ibid.

23. Ibid.

Colossians 2:9.²⁴ In the latter place the apostle, having ostensibly had it revealed to him, inscripturates that in the God-Man, Jesus Christ, all the fulness of the Godhead, θεότης, dwells. NWT with its mutual transposition of the meanings has clearly weakened the thrust of Paul and thereby excised christological deity and substituted mere "divine quality," something attributable to almost anyone in at least some aspect of life. The Witnesses' Jesus is barely above the Liberal Jesus of the nineteenth century.

Pastoral Epistles: "God and Savior" Passages

The writer of the Pastoral Epistles is believed by this investigator to be the Apostle Paul himself. In them he uses the Greek word σωτήρ ten times. The table on page 131 illustrates the diffusion of these occurrences in the Pastorals.

The use of the term "explicitly" in this table ought not to be construed so as to constitute a preclusion that Paul, when speaking of God as Savior, has no thought of Christ being involved. The latter is the task of exegesis. By using "explicitly" the author here wishes to emphasize that grammatically the occurrence of σωτήρ is clearly to be taken with God the Father or Christ.

I Timothy. The apostle in 1:1 designates himself as one sent from Jesus Christ by God our Savior and Christ Jesus our hope. It is acceptable in the sight of this Savior God that prayers should be offered for all men, 2:3. Finally, in 4:10 God who is Savior for all men is especially the Savior of all those who believe. Paul thus describes God as Savior sending messengers, summoning prayers, and saving believers.

NWT inserts no footnote at any of these passages, and justly so. In I Timothy "Savior" is used only of God the Father. No excision of christological deity may be charged at all. To one reading this epistle and observing the term Savior applied to God, the statement in 2:5, "For there is one God," implies that there must correspondingly be but one Savior and He identical with this God.

II Timothy. But for 1:10 the word Savior would have found no place in this

---

24. H. S. Nash, "Θειότης—Θεότης, Rom. i.20; Col. ii.9," *Journal of Biblical Literature* XVIII (1899), pp. 1-34, attempts to remove all distinction between the two words and presents cogent evidence to support his thesis. However, the common meaning of both words in his view is that of deity itself or Godhead, and thus in no way detracts from the argument set forth by the investigator here.

epistle at all. The apostle, describing the sovereign character of Christian salvation—that it is not based upon man's responses but upon God's gracious purpose in Christ before timeless ages—says that it is now manifest through the appearing of Christ our Savior. Again, NWT has rendered σωτήρ with whom it grammatically belongs: in this instance Jesus Christ. The reader who contemplated at I Timothy 2:5 the identification of "one God" with Savior may wonder how it is that Jesus Christ can be designated σωτήρ by the same apostle.

Titus. This third epistle of the Pastorals, although probably the second in order of writing, contains the largest number of instances of σωτήρ. Whereas in I Timothy God is called Savior, and in II Timothy Jesus Christ is called Savior, in the letter to Titus both are called Savior. There is, as it were, almost an ascendancy of ascription of the term.

In 1:3, 4 there is a juxtaposition of God as Savior and Christ as Savior in the same thought structure. NWT runs:

> Whereas in his own due times he made his word manifest in the public announcement with which I was entrusted, under command of our Savior, God; 4 to Titus, a genuine child according to a faith shared in common:
>
> May there be undeserved kindness and peace from God the Father and Christ Jesus our Savior.[25]

Paul calls both Savior in one breath and without any attempt to explain how he can do so doctrinally. And *NWT attempts to draw a distinction that the apostle does not.* In the Greek, verses one to four form the greeting or salutation common to the Pauline corpus. These verses form one unified thought structure and thus a single paragraph. But one will observe that NWT begins a second paragraph, connected, to be sure, by a colon with the former, with the clause designating Jesus as Savior; and thus may be viewed as excisive of christological deity, even though NWT consistently makes double paragraphing of Paul's introductory remarks in each epistle.

In 2:10 the apostle tells slaves to be in subjection to their masters, in order that they "may adorn the teaching of our Savior, God, in all things."[26] Continuing, he speaks of a Christian's present conduct in the light of the future:

25. *New World Translation,* p. 627.
26. Ibid., p. 629.

. . . instructing us to repudiate ungodliness and worldly desires. . .
while we wait for the happy hope and glorious manifestation of the great
God and of our Savior Christ Jesus.[27]

NWT has realized the implication of the construction τὴν μακαρίαν ἐλπ-
ίδα καὶ ἐπιφάνειαν τῆς δόξης τοῦ μεγάλου θεοῦ καὶ σωτῆρος ἡμῶν
χριστοῦ 'Ιησοῦ, for the apparent teaching is that the great God is to be
identified with the Savior Christ. A footnote to verse 13 refers the reader to
the appendix under Titus 2:13.

The appendix commences by citing a sentence from Moulton's *Grammar*
indicating the problem of Titus 2:13 to be an impasse. The Grammar records
five seventh-century A.D. papyri "which attest the translation 'our great God
and Saviour' as current among Greek-speaking Christians."[28] The NWT
translators' comment regarding the latter is highly important: "But these
papyri are all of the late date of the 7th century, hence not at all decisive on
the problem."[29] *This investigator is utterly amazed to observe how NWT
translators can discount so casually "7th century" papyri when the Hebrew
translations constantly cited to support their restoration of "Jehovah" to
the sacred text are themselves much later!*[30]

These papyri are then noted by NWT to contain references to "the mother
of God" and the whole tenor of these "impious pagans" responsible for
these papyri is that of "an everlasting apotheosis." NWT points out that the
formula *"in the name of the Lord and Master Jesus Christ our God and
Savior and of our mistress the holy mother of god, etc.,"* exhibits an echo
found in Ptolemaic formula concerning deified kings.[31] The reasoning of the
Appendix is that apotheosis of a human ruler as "Savior" is pagan. Further,
since Jesus Christ is "a god" and not God, He must be clearly separated
from any reference to God even though designated Savior. Hence,

> The inspired Word of God is against any suggestion that his consecrated
> people borrowed or annexed anything from the impious pagans who
> apotheosized or deified their human rulers. Although the statements at
> John 1:1, 18 "and the Word was a god," and, "the only-begotten

27. Ibid., p. 630.
28. Ibid., pp. 781-82.
29. Ibid.
30. See chap. 3.
31. *New World Translation*, p. 782.

god," would allow for it, yet, grammatically, we render "the great God" as separate from "our Saviour Christ Jesus" at Titus 2:13.[32]

In conclusion those translations agreeing with NWT are cited.

By way of criticism, the investigator must take sharp exception to the entire appendix. First, it drastically fails to meet the real problem: that the ascription of "Savior" is to both God the Father and to Jesus Christ in the same epistle—not to mention the other Pastorals. This matter is completely passed over in silence.

Secondly, the translation, "the happy hope and glorious manifestation of the great God and of our Savior Christ Jesus," interpolates the preposition "of" before "our Savior." This addition to the text implies that the happy hope and manifestation of glory will be an event in which two personages will be seen, God and Christ Jesus. But the contrary may be seen to be true, and for this reason. More than a century ago Granville Sharp formulated a rule concerning the Greek article with nouns connected by καί:

> When the copulative καί connects two nouns of the same case, if the said article ὁ or any of its cases precedes the first of the said nouns or participles, and is not repeated before the second noun or participle, the latter always relates to the same person that is expressed or described by the first noun or participle; i.e., it denotes a farther description of the first-named person.[33]

Applying it to Titus 2:13, τοῦ μεγάλου θεοῦ καὶ σωτῆρος ἡμῶν χριστοῦ Ἰησοῦ, one observes that τοῦ goes with "God" and "Savior." This future expected hope and manifestation is that brought by the advent of the one person "Jesus Christ, the great God and our Savior." Furthermore, if καί be taken as ascensive, the phrase may be rendered "the great God *even* our Savior." Acts 26:30 illustrates the repetition of the article with two nouns connected by καί to indicate *different* persons. Granville Sharp's dogmatic "always" certainly invites a search for exceptions and Matthew 17:1 may be one.

NWT has adduced a disjunction between God and Christ in Titus 2:13, where no necessary disjunction exists in the Greek. The investigator sug-

---

32. Ibid.

33. H. E. Dana and J. R. Mantey, *A Manual Grammar of the Greek New Testament*, p. 147. See also Nigel Turner's comments for and against this rule in his *Syntax*. (vol. III) of *A Grammar of New Testament Greek*, p. 181.

gests emphatically that NWT has allowed a religious tradition, "hoary with age,"[34] to influence the translation. That tradition is none other than the old Arian view of Jesus Christ, that He is more than man but less than God.

The final reference in Titus to God as Savior and Christ as Savior is chapter three, verses four and six. Paul exults in God's kindness and philanthropy manifested in salvation. NWT reads "our Savior God, . . . through Jesus Christ our Savior." Paul again calls both Savior in the same context, even though here he clearly distinguishes the Father from the Son. In verse six "He [God] poured out upon us richly . . . through Jesus Christ our Savior." In Paul's mind God works salvation *through* Jesus Christ. Yet Pauline theology and Christology does not admit of two Saviors. God the Father is Savior; Jesus the Son of God is Savior; both are deity. Again, NWT ignores the problem by silence.

II. *The Deity of the Holy Spirit*

It is the contention of the present writer that the translation "and the Word was God" is justifiable because the New Testament teaches the deity of Christ. The deity of the Holy Spirit is likewise contended to be a doctrine exegeted, not eisegeted, from the same body of Scripture. In this section passages which aid in setting forth the deity of the Holy Spirit, and concomitantly aid in the setting forth of the doctrine of the Trinity, will be observed in NWT in order to demonstrate whether or not there has been employed a principle of excision as with the deity of Christ. First, there will be presented passages bespeaking the Spirit as a person; secondly, passages which assert deity and place the Spirit in a triune context with the Father and the Son.

A Personal Being

The purpose of this section is not to present an exhaustive treatment of New Testament pneumatology, but to present selectively enough passages to demonstrate whether or not the Holy Spirit is a personal being.

The Greek words for Holy Spirit have been observed by this investigator to occur through the New Testament in no single concrete form. Even within a single context the form may differ. One finds τὸ ἅγιον τὸ πνεῦμα, τὸ

---

34. *New World Translation*, p. 6.

πνεῦμα τὸ ἅγιον, τὸ ἅγιον πνεῦμα, ἅγιον πνεῦμα, τὸ πνεῦμα, πνεῦμα and in the oblique cases yet other variations. Although the noun "spirit" is of neuter grammatical gender, there is no justification automatically to register the Holy Spirit as an impersonal influence, no more than to regard the German word for "girl," the neuter *das Mädchen,* as indicating a non-feminine, non-masculine entity.

As one reads NWT he notices that it is always consistently written with no capital letters: "the holy spirit" or "holy spirit." NWT exerted great care to render the arthrous references "the holy spirit" and the anarthrous "holy spirit." In this regard NWT is quite in keeping with the principle set forth in the appendix to John 1:1 concerning the arthrous or anarthrous state of a word. Unfortunately, the style of NWT suffers from so crass a principle for translation. To the English reader a common noun oftentimes just does not sound apropos when the article is excluded. When NWT translates Matthew 1:18, "she was found to be pregnant by holy spirit," Titus 3:15, "but according to his mercy he saved us . . . and through the making of us new by holy spirit," one is confronted with a stylism uncommon to modern English. Thus NWT has aborted an aim enunciated in the Foreword: that Scripture "should be rendered in the same style, in the speech forms current among the people."[35]

In a word, the Witnesses hold that the "holy spirit" is "the invisible active force of Almighty God which moves his servants to do his will."[36] "It" seems as impersonal as the "spirit" of independence which moved the early American patriots.

A critical reader of NWT might haved desired an appendix explaining how it can be that this "invisible active force" does the things ascribed to it in the New Testament. In I Corinthians 12:11 it "wills"; in Mark 13:11 it is seen "speaking"; in Luke 12:12 and parallel passages it "will teach"; in John 16:13 it "will guide" and speak what "he hears"; in verse 7 it is seen as "the helper"; in Acts 13:2 it calls missionaries; in 8:29 it gives command to an evangelist; and in Matthew 1:18 it causes conception.

That the Holy Spirit is personal may be observed further by Jesus' referring to Him as ἐκεῖνος three times in John 16:7-14. The neuter of this demonstrative is ἐκεῖνο and grammatically would agree with τὸ πνεῦμα

---

35. Ibid., p. 9.
36. *What Has Religion Done for Mankind?*, p. 32.

τῆς ἀληθείας of verse thirteen. NWT accounts for this use of the masculine solely on the basis of its gender agreement with ὁ παράκλητος in verse seven. A footnote reads " 'that one,' in the masculine gender, to agree with 'helper' in John 15:26; 16:7."[37] This statement is undoubtedly true. The implication, however, is that a neuter is impersonal.

Ὁ παράκλητος literally means "one called alongside." It is not abstractly "the help" or "the comfort," but actively and concretely "the comforter," and as such can hardly describe an impersonal divine influence. One would at least expect NWT to capitalize "holy spirit" out of high estimation for Jehovah God, whose "invisible active force" it is believed to be.

A Person of the Trinity

In the appendix concerning John 1:1 NWT "disposes of the trinitarian argument" with one sweeping stroke.[38] But if the investigator's presentation of the material in refutation of NWT's contention has any cogency whatever, it may be seen that the "trinitarian argument" has not been disposed of but merely distorted by NWT. The present writer wishes to exhibit three passages which, in his opinion, furnish strong evidence for taking seriously the historic Christian dogma of the Trinity.

The "Great Commission," given by Jesus Christ Himself in Matthew 28:19-20, may be viewed as normative for any consideration of the doctrine of the Trinity. The Witnesses surely accept these words as a genuine saying of Jesus and not as the *Formgeschichte* method concludes, only a saying to be attributed to the early Christian community to establish missionary policy. This investigator concurs with the Witnesses in accepting the Great Commission as genuine. NWT reads:

> Go therefore and make disciples of people of all the nations, baptizing them in the name of the Father and of the Son and of the holy spirit.[39]

The Greek of this verse is very interesting. The baptizing is to be administered in *one* name, not three. This implies some measure of unity. Yet it is to be in the name of *"the* Father" and *"the* Son" and *"the* holy spirit."

---

37. *New World Translation*, p. 335.
38. Ibid., p. 775.
39. Ibid., p. 126.

Granville Sharp's rule does not enter here as at Titus 2:13, because each of these three nouns connected by καί—Father, Son, Holy Spirit—has the article. The reference to Acts 26:30 cited in the discussion under Titus 2:13 contains a construction analogous to this one. In the former Luke says ὁ βασιλεὺς καὶ ὁ ἡγέμων, denoting two persons. In the present passage Jesus uses the article with each noun and thus speaks of three persons. The aspects of unity and three persons in this passage alone may explain why Tertullian designated the Latin word *trinitas* as describing the Godhead. The burden of proof is incumbent upon the NWT translators to demonstrate that such is not the crux. However, one finds no appendix or footnote to Matthew 28:19 offering any explanation whatsoever for this lucid implication for this cardinal Christian dogma.

The next passage is I Corinthians 12:4-6:

> Now there are varieties of gifts, but there is the same spirit; and there are varieties of ministries, and yet there is the same Lord; and there are varieties of operations, and yet is is the same God who performs all the operations in all persons.[40]

NWT cannot here be charged with excisive translation, but it can be charged with observing the same pregnant silence as at Matthew 28. "The same spirit," "the same Lord," and "the same God," are faithful reproductions of the Greek. As in Matthew, there is a triune parallelism of three nouns; and the parallelism is shattered if two of the nouns are of persons and one is merely of an influence.

The Apostle Paul records once more a reference to Father, Son, and Holy Spirit in the same breath. One can hardly deny that at an early date there was a tri-name phraseology in use among Christians. II Corinthians 13:14 suggests what has long been called the "Trinitarian Benediction": "The undeserved kindness of the Lord Jesus Christ and the Love of God and the sharing in the holy spirit be with all of YOU."[41] As in Matthew and in I Corinthians, the article is present before each noun and not after the rule of Granville Sharp. Paul has three entities in view. Furthermore, each article is genitive singular in form: τοῦ, even though "spirit" is neuter, for the masculine and neuter are identical in the genitive singular.

---

40. Ibid., p. 513.
41. Ibid., p. 551.

The outstanding feature of NWT in this verse—beside the lower-case "spirit"—is that τοῦ is translated "of" with Jesus Christ and God, but "in" with "the holy spirit." The English reader invariably will be led to think that a different Greek preposition was used by Paul, and consequently the parallelism which is clear in Greek is weakened in English. The English word "sharing" certainly takes "in" after it, and in that regard may justify NWT for translating "sharing in the holy spirit." However, NWT has not consistently rendered κοινωνία "sharing." In II Corinthians 6:14 it is "fellowship"; 8:4 "share"; 9:13 "contribution"; and in I Corinthians 1:9 it is "partnership"; and 10:16 "sharing." One is reminded of the aim in the Foreword: "To each major word we have assigned one meaning and have held to that meaning as far as the context permitted."[42] In the Corinthian letters alone NWT has assigned to one major word *four* different English meanings. As in the two preceding passages, NWT included no footnote or appendix explaining the obvious implications of the Trinitarian Benediction. But the evidence does indicate that the translators purposely endeavored to excise to some extent the implicit teaching of the Holy Spirit's place in the Trinity.

Conclusion

The purpose of this chapter has been to demonstrate *why* the Word is God. The investigator believes that the material presented from the New Testament amply proves that Scripture witnesses to the Word's deity. In connection with this, the scriptural witness of the Holy Spirit's personality and deity has been presented.

One may see that NWT translated John 1:1 "a god," contrary to the tenor of a Gospel which concludes with the exclamation regarding Jesus, "My Lord and my God!" In Acts 20:28 NWT adopted a conjectural emendation up into the text, an emendation which supported the Witnesses' unitarian view of God and enabled them to turn a "Nelson eye" to a most difficult verse. The appendix of Romans 9:5 showed NWT justifying its translation on the basis of grammar alone, and thus disjoining Jesus from God, when there is on the contrary, great evidence to support the punctuation of the Westcott and Hort text, the basic text of NWT, which allows for the fulness of Christ's deity to be expressed.

42. Ibid., p. 9.

NWT's translation of Colossians 2:9 manifested continuing excisiveness in that in Jesus there dwells merely "divine quality" and not deity itself. The treatment of the Pastorals unveiled an apparently paradoxical situation in which the term "Savior" is applied to both God and Jesus. It was seen that NWT never actually met this problem directly in either its footnotes or appendix.

The second major division of the chapter treated of the Holy Spirit: personality and place in the Trinity. NWT was shown to have excised both, emphasizing the Spirit's impersonal, abstract nature by referring to Him with the neuter pronoun "it" and by using small and not capital letters. The clear passages implying triple personages in the Godhead were passed over in silence by NWT footnote and appendix editors, and in one passage, II Corinthians 13:14, a change in English preposition weakened the force of the grammatical parallelism which exists in the Greek.

The excisive character of the translators of NWT has been much in evidence in this chapter, and this truncation was seen to be "in support of a preferred religious view."[43]

---

43. Ibid., p. 6.

Chapter 6

EXAMPLES OF TRANSLATION

The purpose of this chapter is to present several Greek words and their translation in the NWT in order to observe the accuracy, modernity, and faithfulness of this translation. These words were chosen because they reflect the attitude of the translators regarding the production of a version of the Scriptures. Each word or group of words will be viewed from NWT's rendering and from the Greek text itself. Careful consideration will be given to the influence, if any, of prior doctrinal consideratons on the translation of a word. Also the stated aims of NWT to be faithful to God's Word and to be up-to-date in the selection of an English equivalent for the Greek will be kept in sight.

ΚΕΡΑΣ ΣΩΤΗΡΙΑΣ

In Luke 1:69 NWT translates κέρας σωτηρίας "a mighty savior." A footnote reads, "Literally, . . . a horn of salvation."[1] Κέρας does mean "horn" and σωτηρίας "salvation." One may wonder why the NWT does not simply follow the literal rendering at this point in the interest of producing an avowedly literal translation of the New Testament. It is not following the stated principle when "salvation" is changed into "savior." Since the Witnesses designate Jehovah as "the Almighty God" and Jesus as the "mighty god,"[2] one can observe here an attempt to insert this doctrinal view into an Old Testament quotation. A further indication of the presence of doctrinal bias is in verse 47, where Mary calls God "my Savior"; yet in the present verse when Jesus is called "savior" the word is not capitalized. This calls to mind the God and Savior passages of the Pastoral Epistles and NWT's failure to meet the real issue of one and not two bona fide saviors.

ΑΣΙΑΡΧΗΣ

In Acts 19:31 the NWT renders the plural of Ἀσιάρχης "the commis-

---

1. *New World Translation*, p. 189.
2. *Let God Be True*, pp. 32-33.

sioners of festivals and games.'' The addition of the explanatory, and truly helpful, paraphrase ''of festivals and games'' is unjustifiable on the basis of NWT translation principles. More preferable is a rendering like that of the Authorized Version, ''the chief of Asia,'' or, if desired, simply the transliteration, ''Asiarchs.'' NWT's ''the commissioners of festivals and games'' is not found in Arndt-Gingrich or Liddell-Scott.

ΔΙΑΚΟΝΟΣ

The noun διάκονος is certainly ''a major word'' in the New Testament, appearing 29 times. Literally, the word means ''minister,'' not in the technical sense of today's clergyman, but simply anyone who serves or performs acts of ministering. NWT has translated the word ''minister'' twenty-three times, ''servants'' once, ''those ministering'' twice, and ''ministerial servants'' three times. In John 2:5, 9, τοῖς διακόνοις and οἱ διάκονοι are translated as if they were participles, ''to those ministering'' and ''those ministering'' respectively, and hence, a paraphrase is produced at each place. No doctrinal import attaches to these renderings of this particular Greek word; the way in which it is treated merely demonstrates that NWT is inconsistent in not pursuing its translation principle of noninterpolation.

ΜΟΝΟΓΕΝΗΣ

Traditionally this word has been translated in the English versions ''only begotten.'' Luther's version has *''eingeboren''* in the Johannine passages, and likewise the Latin has *''unigenitus.''* Clearly, then, the idea conveyed is that there has been a ''generation of only one.'' However, the French version has *''unique''* for each of the nine occurrences of μονογενής. The NWT has followed the traditional at this point, reading ''only-begotten'' throughout.

In Luke 7:12; 8;42; and 9:38, two sons and a daughter are designated by NWT as ''only-begotten'' with a footnote reading ''Or, 'the [an, my] only son [one].' '' The Hebrews 11:17 occurrence lacks such an explanatory footnote, as do the instances in John 1:14, 18; 3:16, 18; and I John 4:9. Consistency would demand that the footnote be appended to the Hebrews passage, for it, like that in Luke, refers to human beings. All of the Johannine instances are christological. *If* μονογενής means ''only-begotten," then one may be justified in asking why these Johannine passages do not have "only" as a synonym in the apparatus. The translators believe that,

> It is useless for believers in a trinity to argue that the expression "the firstborn of all creation" does not mean that Jesus Christ was a creation by God. . . . Likewise the corresponding expression "the firstborn of all creation" means he was the first one to be created. He is a creature; he was not coeternal with God. . . . Until his first creation Jehovah God was sonless; by it he became a father. . . . So Jehovah God used nothing female, no mother, by which to produce his first son. For this reason he is rightly called "the only-begotten Son of God. . . ."[3]

The Witnesses have apparently tried to rationalize the historic confessional statement which grew out of the christological controversies of the fourth century—that the Son has been eternally generated by the Father. The Lutheran church historian Neve describes the origin of this idea:

> Origen followed Neo-Platonism, which taught that from the Divine Being proceeds the *Nous*. The Son proceeds from the Father somewhat as the will proceeds from a human being. This procession is expressed in the conception of a generation (*genesis*) of the Son from the Father. But Origen made a larger contribution to the dogma of the Trinity by speaking of an *eternal generation,* the Father *is always begetting* the Son.[4]

Confessedly most positive statements about the nature of the Trinity are woefully inadequate. Origen sought to describe the trinitarian relation as one of everlasting generation and procession. A rather novel view is that presented by J. O. Buswell, Jr. Commenting on μονογενής, he writes:

> It seems that the church fathers of the fourth century, in the heat of the Arian controversy, took the word as somehow connected with the root of the verb *gennao,* which means generate or beget. Thus our English words, "only begotten," are derived from fourth century usage. When the orthodox church fathers were challenged by the Arians, who said that Christ was a created being and who pointed to the word *monogenes* for their evidence, the orthodox fathers did not have the facilities to

---

3. *"New Heavens and a New Earth,"* p. 24.
4. J. L. Neve, *A History of Christian Thought,* I, p. 86.

prove that the word has nothing to do with begetting, but they knew that in the light of other Scriptures, Christ was not created.[5]

Buswell then points out that this notion of Christ's generation from the Father in eternity past, not as an event, but as an unexplainable relationship, has been assumed and passed on in Christian theology from the fourth century to the present.[6] Though it is an interesting analysis, Buswell's position has not gained wide acceptance by evangelical scholars.

His suggestion that the eternal generation of the Son—and the eternal procession of the Spirit—be completely dropped sounds revolutionary. However, he would emphasize strongly that denial of eternal generation is not denial of the absolute essential equality of the Son with the Father; rather, the latter is more firmly advocated by rejecting the former. By concurring with the deliberations of church history that μονογενής means "only-begotten," he believes that orthodox Christians have indirectly aided the cause of subordinationists—as are the Jehovah's Witnesses. The present investigator concludes that by denying "only-begotten" for μονογενής, the eternality of the Son is enhanced and the Witnesses have lost a building block in their Arian edifice.

Careful lexicographical study proves that μονογενής does not derive from γεννάω but from γένος, meaning "kind" or "class." Liddell-Scott lists the general meaning in classical usage as "only, single," with no idea at all of generation.[7] Thayer has "single of its kind, only" and discusses the translation of "only-begotten." Even though he was a unitarian, his comment is very incisive and to the point:

> . . . used of Christ, denotes *the only son of God* or one who in the sense in which he himself is the Son of God has no brethren. He is so spoken of by John not because ὁ λόγος which was ἐνσαρκωθείς in him was eternally generated by God the Father (the orthodox interpretation), or came forth from the being of God just before the beginning of the world (Subordinationism), but because by the incarnation (ἐνσάρκωσις) of the λόγος in him he is of nature or essentially Son of God.[8]

In the best modern lexicon, that of Arndt and Gingrich, μονογενής is

---

5. J. O. Buswell, Jr., *A Systematic Theology of the Christian Religion*, I, pp. 110f.

6. Ibid.

7. H. G. Liddell and R. Scott, *Greek-English Lexicon*, p. 1144.

8. J. Thayer, *Greek-English Lexicon of the New Testament*, pp. 417f.

translated "only" and "unique."[9] Recent translations of the New Testament which concur with this lexicographical evidence and thus in John 3:16 translate μονογενής correctly, are the Revised Standard Version, The New Testament by Charles B. Williams, The New English Bible, and the New American Standard Bible, New Testament.

In view of NWT's consistent translation of μονογενής as "only begotten," its aim towards modernity has not been reached. Unfortunately, the correct meaning of "only," which appeared in footnotes in Luke, was not taken up into the text. This inclusion in the footnotes indicates that the translators were not ignorant of the correct meaning of μονογενής. They do appear to be ignorant of the word's etymology in that they equate "only-begotten" with "only." The old, traditional way was that of "only begotten"; the modern way, based upon sure lexicography, is "only" or "unique."

ΚΟΛΑΣΙΣ

Κόλασις and κολάζω appear in the New Testament twice each; and these four occurrences are in different writers. Matthew and John record the noun and Luke and Peter the verb. NWT translates εἰς κόλασιν αἰώνιον at Matthew 25:46 "everlasting cutting-off." That the enemies of Christ are not consigned to conscious, everlasting torment, the translators make plain in the Appendix on "Gehenna":

> No living animals or human creatures were pitched into Gehenna to be burned alive or tormented. Hence the place could never symbolize an invisible region where human souls are tormented in literal fire and attacked by undying immortal worms for ever and ever. (Isaiah 66:24) . . . Gehenna was used by Jesus and his disciples to symbolize everlasting destruction, annihilation from God's universe, or "second death," an eternal punishment.[10]

In I John 4:18, κόλασις is "restraint" and a footnote reads "Or 'fear has a checking (correction, punishment),' " "To punish" is the rendering of the verb in Acts 4:21 and "to be cut off" in II Peter 2:9 with the footnote "Or, 'be checked.' "

---

9. W. F. Arndt and F. W. Gingrich, *A Greek-English Lexicon to the New Testament and Other Early Christian Literature*, p. 529.

10. *New World Translation*, p. 767.

The root meaning of this word is that of "checking" in the realm of trees—especially the almond—and "chastising of persons." One may rightly assert that corrective punishment may be in view when a writer selects κόλασις. However, such corrective punishment cannot be assumed. Matthew 25:46 demonstrates this with marked finality. If one adopts the Witness doctrine of soul annihilation, how can annihilation be conceived of as corrective? Trench is right to state that κόλασις cannot always be corrective, but may be synonymous with τιμωρία.[11] By choosing "cutting-off" NWT has adopted as applicable to persons what applies to things, and thus underscores annihilation. Interestingly, if the contexts be studied the four verses divide themselves into two pairs: (1) Those in which an everlasting aspect is suggested; and (2) those in which a temporal aspect is suggested. Under the former are the Matthean and Petrine passages with NWT translating each "cut off" to support annihilation. The Lukan and Johannine passages deal with space-time punishment and are rendered "punish" and "restrain" respectively.

The modifier αἰώνιον in Matthew 25:46 further complicates the attempt to eisegete annihilation. Of it Alford wrote:

> Observe, the *same epithet* is used for κόλασις and ζωή—which are here *contraries*—for the ζωή here spoken of is not bare *existence*, which would have *annihilation* for its opposite; but *blessedness* and *reward,* to which *punishment* and *misery* are antagonistic terms.[12]

Although κόλασις and its verb are not "major" words, NWT could have easily and correctly used "punishment" in each of these four instances consistent with the contexts instead of three different meanings as was done. It is evident that a prior doctrinal bias—aversion to everlasting, conscious punishment—prompted the translators to work so skillfully to produce the delicate nuances here set forth. Charles Taze Russell, the first president of the society, was deeply disturbed as a boy by the doctrines of predestination and eternal punishment,[13] and that the NWT translators have remained loyal sons of his is reflected in their treatment of κόλασις.

---

11. Trench, *Synonyms of the New Testament,* p. 25.

12. Alford, *The Greek Testament,* p. 257.

13. Hoekema, *The Four Major Cults,* p. 223.

ΨYXH

As a coin has two sides, so does the doctrine of eternal punishment. The other side is that of immortality. The Witnesses embrace conditional immortality, that is, that to be man is *not* to be immortal; but to be one of Jehovah's tested and proven children is to receive the gift of immortality.

In support of conditional immortality, the NWT translators have adopted the view that man *is* soul and does not merely *possess* a soul. Body and soul are inseparable. Hence, to destroy the body is to destroy or annihilate man's soul. An Appendix to Matthew 2:20 declares this view to be biblical, especially in view of verses cited which indicate that "the creature soul is mortal, destructible."[14] Similar support issues from *"New Heavens and a New Earth"*:

> Death did not mean that a soul taken from heaven and encased in Adam's earthly body would escape and return to heaven and live there immortally. No! . . . for Adam death meant a return to non-existence.[15]

Logically, then, one cannot deny conscious eternal punishment without also denying the immortality of the creature made in God's image.

There are two passages of Scripture which clearly contradict the view enunciated by NWT that man *is* soul. The first is Matthew 10:28, which reads:

> And do not become fearful of those who kill the body but can not kill the soul;[c] but rather be in fear of him that can destroy both soul[c] and body in Gehenna.[d]

This passage asseverates that man has both *a* body and *a* soul. Else how could the Lord say that there is one who is able to kill the body but not the soul? Hoekema well paraphrases the idea of Matthew 10:28 when he writes:

> There is something about you which those who kill you cannot touch! That something is that aspect of man which continues to exist after the body has been lowered into the grave.[16]

Only an unnatural interpretation of this verse could support the Witness

---

14. *New World Translation*, p. 762.
15. *"New Heavens and a New Earth,"* p. 88.
16. Hoekema, *The Four Major Cults*, p. 347.

doctrine that the ψυχή is synonymous for the whole person.

The other passage is Revelation 6:9-10:

> And when he opened the fifth seal, I saw underneath the altar the souls of those slaughtered because of the word of God and because of the witness work which they used to have. And they cried with a loud voice, saying: "Until when, Sovereign Lord holy and true, are you refraining from judging and avenging our blood upon those who dwell on the earth?"

One will search in vain to find here evidence to support the Witness doctrine that man *is* soul, for the Seer of the Apocalypse relates his vision of τὰς ψυχὰς τῶν ἐσφαγμένων. The objects of his sight are "souls," not persons. And to make the disjunction more lucid between man's body and his soul, the Seer employs a partitive genitive—the souls as a part *of* those slaughtered. Furthermore, that these souls are conscious is seen by their crying out to God.

The following statement by I. M. Haldeman serves as the stone to lay to rest the Witness error regarding eternal punishment and conditional immortality:

> If death means the extinction of being, why should life be worse for him [Judas] than any other wicked traitor? No matter how great his guilt, death would end it all. . . .

> Never to have been born means never to have come into existence.

> If death means going out of existence, then never to have been born and to die are equivalent conditions; they mean the same thing—nonexistence.

> Why, then, did the Lord say it would have been good not to come into existence? Why did he not say (seeing the man was born and there was no use in wasting regrets over his birth)—why did he not say, "It will be good for that man when he dies, for when he dies he will then be just as if he had never been born—non-existent"?

> If death means nonexistence, this is what he *ought* to have said.

> To say anything else—if death means non-existence—was utterly meaningless.

> But if death does not mean the end of existence; if death means an eternity of condition; if in this conditioned eternity of being Judas is to suffer for his deed of betrayal, then it is comprehensible why the Son of

God would say it would have been good for that man if he had never been born—if he had never come into existence.

On no other basis is the "Woe to that man" of any intelligent force.[17]

ΤΑΣΣΩ

The manner in which NWT treats the Greek verb τάσσω at Acts 13:48 demonstrates both paraphrase and doctrinal coloring. Καὶ ἐπίστευσαν ὅσοι ἦσαν τεταγμένοι εἰς ζωὴν αἰώνιον reads in NWT, "and all those who were rightly disposed for everlasting life became believers." Lexical meanings for this verb include "to place or put in a fixed spot, to order, determine, or appoint." Luke—who later was to write concerning Lydia, the seller of purple: "whose heart the Lord opened so that she might give heed to the things being spoken by Paul"—here states that in connection with the preaching of the gospel certain Gentiles believed. And they did so because they had been appointed thereunto. The statement of Jesus in John 6:65 comes to mind: "No one is able to come to me unless it has been given to him of the Father."

By inserting the adverb "rightly" before "disposed," NWT has introduced unnecessary paraphrase. That the Gentiles believed indicates that they were disposed to do the right thing.

As a transitive verb, "dispose" denotatively means "to put in order or arrange in sequence." After that it may mean "to influence the mind of" or "to put in a particular place." The first and third meanings are suitable for τάσσω. The second is not. "Dispose" in this sense lays emphasis upon the subject in such a way that the disposition is fully contingent upon the subject. NWT has favored this aspect of "dispose" and has thus made ἦσαν τεταγμένοι mean merely that the gospel message sounded good to these Gentiles who subsequently made up their minds apart from any prior influence from God.

The pluperfect periphrastic ἦσαν τεταγμένοι speaks of an existing result of a past act. The main verb, ἐπίστευσαν, being aorist, the translation should be "and as many as had been appointed unto eternal life believed." Although the author of this prior appointing is not expressed in the context, *there can be no doubt that Luke meant for God to be inferred.* The translators

---

17. I. M. Haldeman, *Millennial Dawnism,* cited in ibid., p. 371.

of NWT wish to have no contact with a God of this nature, and have thus carefully produced a translation which sets forth clearly their doctrinal position.[18]

ΣΤΑΥΡΟΣ

Jesus is recorded in Matthew 10:38 as saying, "And whoever does not accept his torture stake and follow after me is not worthy of me."[19] "Torture stake" stands where "cross" stands in practically every English translation ever produced. A footnote reads, " 'Torture stake'=σταυρός (stau·ros), ℵ B. See Appendix under Matthew 10:38."[20] This dogmatic statement commences the discussion:

> There is no evidence that the Greek word σταυρός meant here a "cross" such as the pagans used as a religious symbol for many centuries before Christ to denote the sun-god.[21]

The classical Greek usage is said to be that of an upright stake or pole or a foundation pile. The verb then meant to fence with poles so as to form a stockade. A criminal to be punished was tied to the *stauros*. The verb *stauroo* appears over forty times in the New Testament and "we have rendered it 'impale,' with the footnote: 'Or, "fasten on a stake or pole." ' "[22]

The Appendix records the synonym of σταυρός, which is ξύλον. The apostles Peter and Paul, it continues, used this word to refer to the torture instrument upon which Jesus was nailed, and "this argues that it was an upright stake without crossbeam, for that is what *xylon* in this special sense means."[23] The Authorized Version usually renders ξύλον "tree" when it refers to Christ's death. There follows a discussion of the Latin translation for σταυρός, *crux*, whose meaning "cross" is said to be late. An illustra-

---

18. There are in Acts only three analogous constructions to 13:48, that is, ἦσαν with the middle-passive form of the perfect participle. They are 4:31; 12:12; and 14:26. *NWT has translated each of these as passive and not middle voice and in doing so has rightly reflected the nearly total demise of the middle voice in the first century.* In 13:48, however, the Witnesses' Arminian orientation has favored the obsolescent middle. In the *Epistle of Barnabas*, at 18:1, certain angels εἰσιν τεταγμένοι (have been appointed) by God. As in Acts 13:48 there is no notion of one "rightly disposing himself" *into* such a relationship.

19. *New World Translation*, p. 62.

20. Ibid.

21. Ibid., p. 768.

22. Ibid.

23. Ibid.

tion of a man impaled upon a *crux* is reproduced from the book *De Cruce Liber Primus* by the sixteenth-century Roman Catholic scholar Justus Lipsius. After mention of the twelfth-century Moses Maimonides, who testifies that the instrument was always a timber uprooted and never a tree still growing, reference is made to *The Cross and Crucifixion* by Hermann Fulda. He states that a simple beam was erected with the criminal's hands tied or nailed above and feet below. Fulda concludes that "Jesus died on a simple deathstake."[24] NWT completes this Appendix by saying:

> The evidence is, therefore, completely lacking that Jesus Christ was crucified on two pieces of timber placed at a right angle. We refuse to add anything to God's written Word by inserting the pagan cross into the inspired Scriptures. . . . This is a revolutionary translation, we admit, but it is the purest one. The passing of time and further archaeological discoveries will be certain to prove its correctness.[25]

The Appendix, in discussing relic worship in Romanism, reveals what probably is the impetus for seeking a different translation for σταυρός. To condemn relic worship is virtuous. But to reject "cross" on that basis is untenable.

The present investigator is not convinced that there is absolutely no evidence to substantiate that σταυρός may have had a crossbeam.[26] However, it must be acknowledged that the presence or absence of such a beam is of little or no importance for Christianity. But it is very important for accuracy in translation. To establish a distinction between σταυρός and ξύλον the writer refers to an article which he formerly wrote discussing these synonymns:

> The distinction between *stauros* and *xulon* is simply this: *xulon* speaks primarily of the material which comprised the cross—wood not metal—whereas *stauros* denotes the position—vertical not horizontal. Testimony from Justin Martyr (second century) and Irenaeus (about 170 A.D.) seems to favor the Latin cross as the form of the cross to which Christ was nailed.[27]

---

24. Ibid., pp. 770-71.

25. Ibid.

26. See Alfred Edersheim, *The Life and Times of Jesus the Messiah*, II, pp. 58ff., and *The Encyclopedia Americana*, VIII, pp. 237f.

27. Robert H. Countess, "Study in New Testament Synonyms," *Biblical Viewpoint*, p. 43. Additional testimony favoring a crossbar on the stake may be found in Merrill F. Unger,

Whether a single beam or a cross is inconsequential. But NWT does err in using "impale" for the verb σταυρόω *as used in the New Testament,* for "impale" means to pierce through with a pole or stick and is misleading to the English reader. It is certain that Jesus and the malefactors were not *impaled,* pierced through. They were nailed and/or tied to the timber. "Affix" or "fasten" to a beam would have been more accurate.

Conclusion

This chapter sought to present specific examples beyond those already investigated in detail in previous chapters of this dissertation to show if the translators were consistent in adhering to their aims enunciated in the Foreword of NWT.

In the paraphrase of Luke 1:69, "a mighty savior," doctrinal presupposition appears markedly to have influenced the choice of words. Literally, "horn of salvation," referring to Jesus, was transformed into a personalized form, "a mighty savior." In line with Witness doctrine Jesus is dissociated from Jehovah God, the Almighty Savior. The treatment of 'Ασιάρχης is a good example of translation become commentary. It would have been more nearly proper to have placed "the commissioners of festivals and games" in a footnote.

Translating μονογενής as "only-begotten" in the text, the translators failed to be accurate, modern, and unbiased. "Only-begotten" gave way in the Lukan footnotes to "only," a more accurate and modern translation. The preference for the idea of begetting by the translators as touching Jesus had in its favor that low view of Him which pictures His person as merely the first of God's many creatures. Jesus is for the Witnesses a sort of elder brother to be looked up to rather than deity to be worshiped.

With the discussion of κόλασις, the Witness doctrine of the afterlife presented itself. The selection of "cutting off" reflected the translators' belief in soul annihilation, whereas, regarding persons, κολάζω contains the ideas of chastisement. This word was not one of NWT's major words, but, even so, one could wish that NWT had consistently used "punishment" rather than three different English words. The treatment of ψυχή revealed

---

Unger's Bible Dictionary, p. 227, and the *Schaff-Herzog Encyclopedia of Religious Knowledge,* under "Cross."

a somewhat naïve attitude among the translators, because the thrust of Matthew 10:28 and Revelation 6:9-10 cannot seriously be construed to teach that man is soul. Regarding τάσσω in Acts 13:48, other doctrinal bias presented itself—that man is capable of believing the gospel apart from God's prevenient influence which effects man's salvation. Furthermore, NWT has failed to convey the force of the pluperfect periphrastic.

The use of σταυρός demonstrated their zeal for obliterating any vestige of "paganism" from Scripture. The idea and word itself, to the translators, convey ancient immoral overtones and Romish relic worship. On the basis of demonstrably inconclusive evidence the translators dogmatically concluded that σταυρός had, and could have had, no crossbeam. However, it was noted that biblical Christianity has no vested interest in the shape of Christ's σταυρός. The NWT rendering, "impale," conveys the idea of a thrusting through with a sharp stick and, therefore, is an inaccurate choice.

These examples of translation from NWT have been presented in the light of the aims of the "Foreword," and, therefore, the present investigator believes NWT to be at these places inconsistent with its self-stated aims.

Chapter 7

SUMMARY AND CONCLUSIONS

It was noted in the introduction to chapter 1 that NWT is the first of the cults to produce *in toto* its own translation of the New Testament. In view of this uniqueness of NWT this investigator has had the opportunity of discovering to what lengths a group may go in order to support its doctrines. The *New World Translation of the Christian Greek Scriptures* thoroughly deserves to be regarded as a unique translation, because it reflects more clearly than any other English translation a particular doctrinal slant.

I. *Summary*

The problem which elicited this dissertation was the claims by NWT itself—that it is an honest, reasonable, consistent, modern, unbiased, and scholarly translation. In order to verify or dispose of these claims it was necessary to enter into a study of text and textual principles, the Divine Name, θεός, the deity of Christ and the Holy Spirit, paraphrase, and anti-traditionalism.

Chapter 2 treated of NWT's text and principles of textual criticism. The names and academic qualifications of a version's translators, a matter of interest to the reader, were unfortunately not able to be discovered. The chosen basic text of Westcott and Hort was observed to have been followed in the main. At the points where "Jehovah" was inserted, the various Hebrew translations listed in Table I were cited for support. NWT was credited with its attempt to provide a *criticus apparatus* instead of saying "Other ancient authorities read. . . ."

Regarding textual principles, NWT advocated what may be termed a *principle* of *non-interpolation*. Refusal to add anything to God's Word is thoroughly consistent with the high view of inspiration which the Foreword of NWT enunciates. Another was consistency in rendering one Greek word with the same English word where contextually possible. Weighing rather than counting manuscripts appeared to have been a guide in preparing NWT. Hence, certain poorly attested passages found in some English versions were omitted.

Chapter 3 faced the challenge of NWT that Jehovah be "restored" to the pages of the New Testament. A detailed presentation of the Foreword's discussion of the matter set forth the reasons for attempting such a restoration. The Hebrew translations presented in tabular form in chapter 2 were then discussed in view of the principle by which the restoration was to have been made. It was noted in support of NWT's position that some evidence exists for believing that the tetragrammaton *may have been* in the autographa of LXX. The crux was not that of the tetragrammaton in the LXX, but the big gap between LXX and the New Testament autographa *and the absolute lack of any evidence whatsoever to prove that the tetragrammaton existed in the New Testament. The reader must always remember how tenuous extrapolative reasoning is, because extrapolation is never* as good as tangible—in this case, *manuscript*—evidence.

The section of chapter 3 treating of Jesus' identification with Jehovah probed to the very core of NWT. Restoration of the Divine Name was clearly seen to have been a means by which the Witnesses' doctrine of Christ was furthered. The employment by NWT of its established principle for restoring the Divine Name was demonstrated through Tables II, III, and IV to have been inconsistently applied. The verses discussed, especially I Peter 2:3, were presented on the basis of the hypothetical correctness of NWT's contention: that the tetragrammaton existed in the autographa. On the translators' own principle there was demonstrated to be textual identification of Jesus with Jehovah.

Chapter 4 concerned itself primarily with the Greek word for God, θεός. The presentation of NWT's John 1:1 appendix set forth the justification for rendering the traditionally Christ-deity verse "and the Word was a god." NWT established a grammatical principle by which θεός="a god" and ὁ θεός="God." The investigator observed that the NWT notion of Jesus' being a good god implies polytheism. The inclusion of a study on the Greek article illustrated that particle's flexibility and genius. And the inclusion of Colrule, while approving the latter, lent new impetus to study of the article and its importance for text, grammar, and translation. Table V, concerning θεός, demonstrated NWT's handling of this word throughout the New Testament and provided a basis for judging NWT's *faithlessness* to its own principle regarding the arthrous and anarthrous noun.

The fifth chapter asked whether or not NWT was characterized by excision of the deity of Jesus Christ and of the Holy Spirit in translation. The method adopted to ascertain this was that of exegeting certain verses whose testimony for deity is quite forceful. These included John 1:1, Acts 20:28, and Romans 9:5. To each of these there was an appendix in NWT explaining the preferred translation—which always fell on the side which makes Christ less than truly God. The Holy Spirit's deity was presented in connection with His personality and inclusion in forcefully clear trinitarian passages, such as Matthew 28:19-20, I Corinthians 12:4-6, and II Corinthians 13:14.

The sixth chapter sought to present several Greek words and their translation in NWT in order to observe this version's accuracy, modernity, and failure to follow its stated principles. Special consideration was given to the Witnesses' doctrine of conditional immortality and punishment by annihilation.

II. *Conclusions*

One of the conclusions of chapter 2 which is common to every chapter is *that NWT has been sharply unsuccessful in keeping doctrinal considerations from influencing the actual translation.* The *lateness* of the Hebrew translations must be viewed as alone devastating to the NWT contention regarding support for the Divine Name. The absolute absence of any extant New Testament manuscript—out of over 13,000 available—containing the Divine Name in tetragrammaton form demolishes whatever force of presupposition yet remains. The textual principles in NWT are few, and two are very dangerous: that of interpolation and that of rationalism. These were observable in the following chapters. The NWT basic objection to the historic Christian doctrine of the Trinity is manifestly that to man such a doctrine is incomprehensible and irrational.

Chapter 3 concluded that the "restoration" of the Divine Name is a misnomer and ought rather to be designated the *"insertion* of the Divine Name." The assumption that the original LXX possessed the tetragrammaton rests on second or first century B.C. fragments of Papyrus Fouad 266, and cannot serve as the conclusive indicator. Exegesis of I Peter 2:3 demonstrated that Jesus may be textually identified with Jehovah, an abhorrent thought to NWT. Likewise, I Peter 3:15 shows an Old Testament quotation in which "Jehovah" is used with reference to the Son of God. The "piercing" in John 10:37 indicated a mistranslation of the Hebrew in Zechariah

12:10, which error served to support NWT's bias against Jesus' person. The excerpt from the investigator's correspondence with the Watchtower Society regarding I Peter 2:3 manifested the Witnesses' refusal forthrightly to face the issue of textual identification which is here incontestable.

Chapter four's conclusions regarding the handling of θεός indicated that NWT's translators poorly understood the Greek article, and that their principle θεός="a god," ὁ θεός="God" is not legitimate. The chapter concluded that, on the basis of NWT's principle, the translators were *94 percent of the time unfaithful to their own translation principle,* an achievement that hardly commends a translation to the serious reader. The investigator believes that future study is needed to establish further "Colrule," whose right to a place in Greek grammars seems conclusive. It would be interesting to see a confrontation of NWT translators with Colrule, for they are apparently ignorant of it. Finally, the discussion of the first chapter of John revealed that θεός occurs eight times in the first eighteen verses, and is anarthrous six times. Yet NWT rendered these six instances "god" only twice. The investigator concludes that the NWT principle of the arthrous or anarthrous θεός is merely a mask, for arbitrary judgment appears to be the criterion. The chapter concluded that the translation "And the Word was God" is justified and proper and thoroughly consonant with the whole of John's Gospel, which concludes with Thomas' confession, "My Lord and my God!"

Chapter 5 demonstrated *why* the Word is God. The investigator is fully convinced that it is so because the deity of the Word is the teaching of the Scriptures. The treatment of Romans 9:5 illustrated NWT's consistent "preferred religious view" that Jesus is not to be identified with God. Colossians 2:9 showed that NWT could take two Greek words and translate the stronger with a weaker English word and the weaker Greek word with a stronger English one. The reason, of course, was to detract from christological deity. The "Savior-God" passages in the Pastorals manifested NWT's refusal to face squarely the real issue—that "one God" and "one Savior" are in some way identical.

Three select passages proved that the historic trinitarian doctrine rests upon scriptural implications and not traditions "hoary with age." Scripture, and not systematic theology, demonstrates the Holy Spirit's personality, deity, and trinitarian status.

Chapter 6 presented enough examples from NWT to show that, often enough, paraphrase was preferred over the literal and more simple rendering. Especially was the unjustifiable paraphrasing evidenced regarding Ἀσιάρχης and διάκονος. Imprecise translation was noted in connection with the words μονογενής and σταυρός, while doctrinal bias intensely influenced the translators' attitude toward κόλασις, ψυχή, and τάσσω.

In the opinion of this investigator the *New World Translation of the Christian Greek Scriptures* must be viewed as a radically biased piece of work. At some points it is actually dishonest. At others it is neither modern nor scholarly. And interwoven throughout its fabric is inconsistent application of its own principles enunciated in the Foreword and Appendix. The present writer strongly recommends that no confrontation between a Jehovah's Witness and Christian be based solely upon NWT; such a confrontation would be grounded upon a biased and manipulated foundation.

From a purely literary standpoint NWT suffers from a woodenness of style that makes sustained reading of it a chore. This liability alone outweighs the sum of NWT's modest assets.

Bibliography

A. *Books*

Alford, Henry. *The Greek Testament.* 2 vols. Chicago: Moody Press, 1958.

Arndt, William F., and F. Wilbur Gingrich. *A Greek-English Lexicon of the New Testament and Other Early Christian Literature.* Chicago: University of Chicago Press, 1957.

Basis for Belief in a New World. Brooklyn: Watchtower Bible and Tract Society, 1953.

Berkhof, L. *Systematic Theology.* Grand Rapids: Eerdmans, 1959.

Bruder, Caroli Hermanni. *Concordance Novi Testamenti Graeci.* Lipsiae: Sumptibus Ernesti Bredtil, 1867.

Bultmann, Rudolph. *Glauben und Verstehen.* Tübingen: Verlag J. C. B. Mohr, 1933.

Burkitt, F.C. and Vincent Taylor. *Fragments of the Books of Kings According to the Translation of Aquila.*

Buswell, J. O., Jr. *A Systematic Theology of the Christian Religion.* 2 vols. Grand Rapids: Zondervan Publishing House, 1962.

Chase, Alston H., and Henry Phillips, Jr. *A New Introduction to Greek.* 3rd ed. Cambridge, Mass.: Harvard University Press, 1964.

Confession of Faith, Larger Catechism, Shorter Catechism, Directory of Public Worship, Presbyterial Church Government. Edinburgh: William Blackwood and Sons Ltd., 1959.

Dana, H. E., and J. R. Mantey. *A Manual Grammar of the Greek New Testament.* New York: The Macmillan Company, 1927.

Dodd, C. H. *The Bible and the Greeks.* London: Hodder and Stoughton, 1935.

Dupont-Sommer, A. *The Essene Writings from Qumran*. Trans. G. Vermes. New York: The World Publishing Company, 1962.

Edersheim, Alfred. *The Life and Times of Jesus the Messiah*. 2 vols. Grand Rapids: Wm. B. Eerdmans Publishing Company, 1959.

Funk, Robert W. (translator and reviser). *A Greek Grammar of the New Testament and Other Early Christian Literature*. Chicago: The University of Chicago Press, 1961.

Gillespie, G. K. *The Englishman's Greek Concordance of the New Testament*. 9th ed. London: Samuel Bagster and Sons, 1903.

Gregory, Caspar René. *The Canon and Text of the New Testament*. New York: Charles Scribner's Sons, 1907.

Hatch, Edwin, and Henry A. Redpath. *A Concordance to the Septuagint and the Other Greek Versions of the Old Testament*. 2 vols. Oxford: Clarendon Press, 1897.

Hodge, Charles. *Commentary on the Epistle to the Romans*. Grand Rapids: Wm. B. Eerdmans Publishing Company, 1886.

Hoekema, Anthony A. *The Four Major Cults*. Grand Rapids: Wm. B. Eerdmans Publishing Company, 1963.

Kahle, Paul E. *The Cairo Geniza*. London: Oxford University Press, 1947.

Keil, C. F., and F. Delitzsch. *The Twelve Minor Prophets*, vol. II of *Biblical Commentary on the Old Testament*. 25 vols. Trans. James Martin. Grand Rapids. Wm. B. Eerdmans Publishing Company, 1950.

Kittel, Gerhard. *Theological Dictionary of the New Testament*. Trans. Geoffrey W. Bromiley. Grand Rapids: Wm. B. Eerdmans Publishing Company, 1964–1974.

Lauterbach, J. Z. *Substitutes for the Tetragrammaton*. Philadelphia: American Academy for Jewish Research, Proceedings, 1931.

Let God Be True. Brooklyn: Watchtower Bible and Tract Society, 1952.

Liddell, Henry George, and Robert Scott. *Greek-English Lexicon*. Ed. Henry Stuart Jones. Oxford: Clarendon Press, 1940.

Martin, Walter R., and Norman H. Klann. *Jehovah of the Watchtower*. New York: Biblical Truth Publishing Society, Inc., 1953.

Metzger, Bruce M. *The Text of the New Testament, Its Transmission, Corruption, and Restoration.* New York: Oxford University Press, 1964.

Middleton, Thomas Fanshaw. *The Doctrine of the Greek Article.* Cambridge: J. and J. J. Deighton, 1833.

Moulton, W. F., and A. S. Geden. *A Concordance to the Greek New Testament.* 4th ed. Edinburgh: T. and T. Clark, 1963.

Neve, J. L. *A History of Christian Thought.* 2 vols. Philadelphia: The Muhlenberg Press, 1946.

"New Heavens and a New Earth." Brooklyn Watchtower Bible and Tract Society, 1953.

New World Translation of the Christian Greek Scriptures. Brooklyn: Watchtower Bible and Tract Society, Inc., 1950.

New World Translation of the Holy Scriptures. Brooklyn: Watchtower Bible and Tract Society of New York, Inc., 1961.

Nestle, Eberhard, and Kurt Aland. *Novum Testamentum Graece.* 24th ed. Stuttgart: Privilegierte Württembergische Bibelanstalt, 1960.

Rahlfs, Alfred. *Septuaginta.* 2 vols. 7th ed. Stuttgart: Württembergische Bibelanstalt, 1935.

Robertson, A. T. *Grammar of the Greek New Testament in the Light of Historical Research.* Nashville: Broadman Press, 1934.

Rushdoony, Rousas J. *By What Standard? An Analysis of the Philosophy of Cornelius Van Til.* Philadelphia: The Presbyterian and Reformed Publishing Company, 1959.

Stuermann, Walter E. *The Jehovah's Witnesses and the Bible.* Tulsa, Okla.: University of Oklahoma, 1955.

Swete, Henry Barclay. *An Introduction to the Old Testament in Greek.* Cambridge: University Press, 1902.

Thackeray, H. St. J. (trans.). *Josephus, Jewish Antiquities.* New York: G. P. Putnam's Sons (Loeb Classical Library), 1930.

Thayer, J. H. *Greek-English Lexicon of the New Testament.* Grand Rapids: Zondervan Publishing House, 1962.

The Encyclopedia Americana. 30 vols. New York: Americana Corporation, 1961.

The Holy Bible. American Standard Version. New York: Thomas Nelson and Sons, 1961.

The Holy Bible. Authorized King James Version. Oxford: The University Press, [1611].

The Holy Bible. Revised Standard Version. New York: Thomas Nelson and Sons, 1952.

The Kingdom Is at Hand. Brooklyn: Watchtower Tract and Bible Society, 1944.

Tillich, Paul. *The Courage to Be.* New Haven: Yale University Press, 1952.

Turner, Nigel. *Syntax.* Vol. III of *A Grammar of New Testament Greek.* Edinburgh: T. and T. Clark, 1963.

Vos, Geerhardus. *Biblical Theology, Old and New Testaments.* Grand Rapids: Wm. B. Eerdmans Publishing Company, 1959.

Westcott, B. F. *The Gospel According to St. John.* Grand Rapids: Wm. B. Eerdmans Publishing Company, 1958.

What Has Religion Done for Mankind? Brooklyn: Watchtower Bible and Tract Society, 1951.

Winer, George B. *A Grammar of the Idiom of the New Testament.* Trans. Gottlieb Luneman. 7th ed. Andover, Mass.: Warren F. Draper, 1886.

B. *Periodicals*

Byington, Stephen T. "Review of Jehovah's Witnesses," *The Christian Century* LXVII (November 1, 1950), p. 1295.

Colwell, E. C. "A Definite Rule for the Use of the Article in the Greek New Testament," *Journal of Biblical Literature* LII (1933), pp. 12-21.

Countess, Robert H. "Study in New Testament Synonyms," *Biblical Viewpoint,* 1964, pp. 41-44.

Eakin, Frank. "The Greek Article in First and Second Century Papyri," *The American Journal of Philology* XXXVII (1916), pp. 334-340.

Gildersleeve, B. L. "On the Article with Proper Names," *The American Journal of Philology* XI (1890), p. 485.

Griffiths, J. Gwyn. "A Note on the Anarthrous Predicate in Hellenistic Greek," *The Expository Times* LXII (July, 1951), pp. 314-16.

Metzger, Bruce. "On the Translation of John i.i," *The Expository Times* LXIII (1951–52), pp. 125-60.

————. "The Jehovah's Witnesses and Jesus Christ," *Theology Today* X (April, 1953), pp. 65-85.

Robertson, A. T. "The Greek Article and the Deity of Christ," *Expositor* VIII (1921), pp. 182-88.

Waddell, W. D. "The Tetragrammaton in the LXX," *Journal of Theological Studies* XLV (1944), pp. 158-61.

Walker, Norman. "The Writing of the Divine Name in the Mishna," *Vetus Testamentum* I (1951), pp. 309-10.

Watchtower Bible and Tract Society. "How Bible Translators Work," *The Christian Century* LXVIII (May 9, 1951).

C. *Unpublished Materials*

Funk, Robert W. "The Syntax of the Greek Article: Its Importance for Critical Pauline Problems." Unpublished Doctoral thesis, Vanderbilt University Divinity School, Nashville, Tenn., 1953.

Skilton, John H. "The Translation of the New Testament into English, 1881–1950: Studies in Language and Style. Unpublished Doctoral thesis, The University of Pennsylvania, Philadelphia, Pa., 1961.

Van Til, Cornelius. "Christianity in Conflict." Unpublished class syllabus, Westminster Theological Seminary, Philadelphia, Pa., 1964. (Mimeographed.)

Other Sources

Personal Correspondence of the Author

Watchtower Bible and Tract Society. Unsigned letter, Brooklyn, N. Y. September 27, 1963.

Watchtower Bible and Tract Society. Unsigned letter, Brooklyn, N. Y. August 16, 1965.

Appendix

TABLE I

HEBREW TRANSLATIONS OF THE NEW TESTAMENT

Symbol	Name	Date
J[1]	*Matthew in Hebrew*	1555
J[2]	*Matthew*	1385
J[3]	*Matthew and Hebrews*	1537
J[4]	*Matthew*	1551
J[5]	*Liturgical Gospels*	1574
J[6]	*Liturgical Gospels*	1576
J[7]	*Greek Scriptures*	1599
J[8]	*Greek Scriptures*	1661
J[9]	*Gospels*	1639
J[10]	*Gospels*	1800
J[11]	*Greek Scriptures*	1817
J[12]	*Greek Scriptures*	1831
J[13]	*Greek Scriptures*	1838
J[14]	*Greek Scriptures*	1846
J[15]	*Luke, Acts, Romans,* and *Hebrews*	1855
J[16]	*Greek Scriptures*	1866
J[17]	*Greek Scriptures*	1877
J[18]	*Greek Scriptures*	1885
J[19]	John	1930
J[20]	*A Concordance to the Greek Testament*[1]	1897
J[21]	*The Emphatic Diaglott*[2]	1864

1. W. F. Moulton and A. S. Geden. "Principally in the Scripture references under ΘΕΟΣ and ΚΥΡΙΟΣ it intersperses parts of the Hebrew text containing the tetragrammaton (יהוה) to which the Greek text refers or from which it makes a quotation." *New World Translation, ibid.,* p. 33.

2. *Loc. cit.* A new, emphatic version, an interlinear, this is the work of Benjamin Wilson using J. J. Griesbach's recension, and it is apparently the first American translation to insert the name "Jehovah" into the English text of the New Testament.

TABLE II

ΚΎΡΙΟΣ **IN THE NEW TESTAMENT WHERE** יהוה **APPEARS IN THE OLD TESTAMENT**[3]

| | | NWT Translation | |
Book	Reference	"Jehovah"	"Lord"
Matthew	3:3	X	
	4:7	X	
	4:10	X	
	21:9	X	
	21:42	X	
	22:37	X	
	22:44	X	
Mark	12:29	XX	
Luke	4:18	X	
	4:19	X	
John	12:38	X	
Acts	2:20	X	
	2:21	X	
	2:25	X	
	3:22	X	
	4:26	X	
	7:49	X	
	15:17	X	
Romans	4:8	X	
	9:28	X	
	9:29	X	
	11:34	X	
	15:11	X	
I Corinthians	3:20	X	
	10:26	X	
II Timothy	2:19	X	
Hebrews	7:21	X	
	8:8	X	
	8:9	X	
	8:10	X	
	8:11	X	

3. This and table III are based upon *A Concordance to the Greek Testament* by W. F. Moulton and A. S. Geden.

TABLE II (continued)

		NWT Translation	
Book	*Reference*	*"Jehovah"*	*"Lord"*
	10:30	X	
	12:5	X	
	12:6	X	
	13:6	X	
I Peter	1:25	X	
	2:3		X
	3:12	XX	
	3:15		X

TABLE III

ΘΕΟΣ IN THE NEW TESTAMENT WHERE יהוה APPEARS IN THE OLD TESTAMENT

		NWT Translation		
Book	*Reference*	*"Jehovah"*	*"Lord"*	*"God"*
Matthew	4:4	X		
John	6:45	X		
Romans	4:3	X		
	11:2			X
	11:8			X
Hebrews	2:13	X		
	9:20			X
	12:29			X
James	2:23	X		

TABLE IV

"JEHOVAH'S" IN THE MAIN TEXT OF NWT

Book	Actual occurrence of יהוה in quotation behind ΚΥΡΙΟΣ & ΘΕΟΣ	NWT Translation: Based on יהוה	Based on no יהוה	Total "Jehovah's"
Matthew	8	7	11	18
Mark	2	2	7	9
Luke	2	2	34	36
John	2	1	4	5
Acts	7	7	45	52
Romans	8	5	14	19
I Corinthians	2	2	13	15
II Corinthians			10	10
Galatians			1	1
Ephesians			6	6
Colossians			6	6
I Thessalonians			4	4
II Thessalonians			3	3
II Timothy	1	1	3	4
Hebrews	12	9	3	12
James	1		13	13
I Peter	5	3		3
II Peter			6	6
Jude			3	3
Revelation			12	12

TABLE V

THE TRANSLATION OF ΘΕΟΣ IN NWT

MATTHEW

Arthrous (40)		*Anarthrous* (11)	
Source	*NWT*	*Source*	*NWT*
1:23	God	3:16	God
3:9	God	4:4	God
4:3	God	5:9	God
6	God	6:24	God
7	God	12:28	God
10	God	14:33	God
5:8	God	19:26	God
34	God	27:43	God
6:8	God	46 (2)	God
30	God	54	God
8:29	God		
9:8	God		
12:4	God		
28	God		
15:3	God		
4	God		
6	God		
31	God		
16:16	God		
23	God		
19:6	God		
24	God		
21:31	God		
43	God		
22:16	God		
21 (2)	God		
29	God		
31	God		
32 (4)	God		
37	God		
23:22	God		
26:61	God		
63 (2)	God		
27:40	God		
43	God		

TABLE V (continued)
MARK

Arthrous (42)		Anarthrous (6)	
Source	*NWT*	*Source*	*NWT*
1:14	God	10:27	God
15	God	11:22	God
24	God	12:26 (2)	God
2:7	God	27	a God
12	God	15:39	God
26	God		
3:11	God		
35	God		
4:11	God		
26	God		
30	God		
5:7 (2)	God		
7:8	God		
9	God		
13	God		
8:33	God		
9:1	God		
47	God		
10:9	God		
14	God		
15	God		
18	God		
23	God		
24	God		
25	God		
27	God		
12:14	God		
17 (2)	God		
24	God		
26 (2)	God		
29	God		
30	God		
34	God		
13:19	God		
14:25	God		
15:34 (2)	God		
43	God		
16:19	God		

TABLE V (continued)
LUKE

Arthrous (109)		Anarthrous (13)	
Source	NWT	Source	NWT
1:6	God	1:35	God
8	God	78	God
16	God	2:14	God
19	God	40	God
26	God	52	God
30	God	3:2	God
32	God	11:20	God
37	God	12:21	God
47	God	16:13	God
64	God	20:36	God
68	God	37 (2)	God
2:13	God	38	God
20	God		
28	God		
38	God		
3:6	God		
8	God		
38	God		
4:3	God		
8	God		
9	God		
12	God		
34	God		
4:41	God		
43	God		
5:1	God		
21	God		
25	God		
26	God		
6:4	God		
12	God		
20	God		
7:16 (2)	God		
28	God		
29	God		
30	God		
8:1	God		
10	God		

TABLE V (continued)

LUKE *(continued)*

Source	NWT	Source	NWT
11	God		
21	God		
28	God		
39	God		
9:2	God		
11	God		
20	God		
27	God		
43	God		
60	God		
62	God		
10:9	God		
11	God		
27	God		
11:20	God		
28	God		
42	God		
49	God		
12:6	God		
8	God		
9	God		
20	God		
24	God		
28	God		
13:13	God		
18	God		
20	God		
28	God		
29	God		
14:15	God		
15:10	God		
16:15 (2)	God		
16	God		
17:15	God		
17:18	God		
20 (2)	God		
21	God		
18:2	God		
4	God		

TABLE V (continued)
LUKE *(continued)*

Source	NWT	Source	NWT
7	God		
11	God		
13	God		
16	God		
17	God		
19	God		
24	God		
25	God		
27	God		
29	God		
43 (2)	God		
19:11	God		
37	God		
20:21	God		
25 (2)	God		
37	the God		
21:31	God		
22:16	God		
18	God		
69	God		
70	God		
23:35	God		
40	God		
47	God		
51	God		
24:19	God		
53	God		

JOHN

Arthrous (61)		Anarthrous (20)	
1:1	God	1:1	a god
2	God	6	God
29	God	12	God
1:34	God	1:13	God
36	God	18 (2)	God, the . . . god
49	God	3:2	God
51	God	21	God
3:2	God	6:45	God
3	God	8:54	God

TABLE V (continued)

JOHN *(continued)*

Source	NWT	Source	NWT
5	God	9:16	God
16	God	33	God
17	God	10:33	a god
18	God	34	gods
33	God	35	gods
34 (2)	God	13:3	God
36	God	16:30	God
4:10	God	19:7	God
24	God	20:17 (2)	God
5:18 (2)	God		
25	God		
42	God		
44	God		
6:27	God		
28	God		
29	God		
33	God		
46	God		
69	God		
7:17	God		
8:40	God		
41	God		
42 (2)	God		
47 (3)	God		
9:3	God		
24	God		
29	God		
31	God		
10:35	God		
36	God		
11:4 (2)	God		
22 (2)	God		
27	God		
40	God		
52	God		
12:43	God		
13:3	God		
31	God		
32	God		

TABLE V (continued)
JOHN (continued)

Source	NWT	Source	NWT
14:1	God		
16:2	God		
17:3	God		
20:28	God		
31	God		
21:19	God		

ACTS

Arthrous (153		Anarhrous (10)	
1:3	God	5:29	God
2:11	God	39	God
17	God	7:40	gods
22 (2)	God	55	God
23	God	12:22	A god's
24	God	14:15	the . . . God
30	God	17:23	God
32	God	19:26	gods
33	God	20:21	God
36	God	28:6	a god
39	God		
47	God		
3:8	God		
9	God		
13 (2)	God		
15	God		
18	God		
3:21	God		
22	God		
25	God		
26	God		
4:10	God		
19 (2)	God		
21	God		
24	God		
31	God		
5:4	God		
30	God		
31	God		
32	God		

TABLE V (continued)

ACTS (continued)

Source	NWT	Source	NWT
6:2	God		
7	God		
11	God		
7:2	God		
6	God		
7	God		
9	God		
17	God		
20	divinely		
25	God		
32	God		
35	God		
37	God		
42	God		
43	the god		
45	God		
46 (2)	God		
55	God		
56	God		
8:10	God		
12	God		
14	God		
20	God		
21	God		
9:20	God		
10:2 (2)	God		
3	God		
4	God		
15	God		
22	God		
28	God		
31	God		
33	God		
34	God		
38 (2)	God		
40	God		
41	God		
42	God		
46	God		

TABLE V (continued)

ACTS *(continued)*

Source	NWT	Source	NWT
11:1	God		
9	God		
17 (2)	God		
18 (2)	God		
23	God		
12:5	God		
23	God		
13:5	God		
7	God		
16	God		
17	God		
21	God		
23	God		
26	God		
30	God		
31	God		
36	God		
37	God		
43	God		
46	God		
14:11	the gods		
22	God		
26	God		
27	God		
15:4	God		
7	God		
8	God		
10	God		
12	God		
14	God		
19	God		
16:10	God		
14	God		
17	God		
25	God		
34	God		
17:13	God		
24	God		
27	God		

TABLE V (continued)

ACTS (continued)

Source	NWT	Source	NWT
29	God		
30	God		
18:7	God		
11	God		
13	God		
26	God		
19:8	God		
11	God		
37	goddess		
20:24	God		
27	God		
28	God		
32	God		
21:19	God		
20	God		
22:3	God		
14	God		
23:1	God		
3	God		
4	God		
24:14	God		
15	God		
16	God		
26:6	God		
8	God		
18	God		
20	God		
22	God		
29	God		
27:23	God		
24	God		
25	God		
35	God		
28:15	God		
23	God		
28	God		
31	God		

TABLE V (continued)
ROMANS

Arthrous (114)		Anarthrous (39)	
Source	NWT	Source	NWT
1:8	God	1:1	God
9	God	4	God
10	God	7 (2)	God
19 (2)	God	16	God
21	God	17	God
23	God	18	God
24	God	21	God
25	God	2:17	God
26	God	3:5	God
28 (2)	God	18	God
32	God	21	God
2:2	God	22	God
3	God	4:2	God
4	God	17	God
5	God	7:25	God
11	God	8:7	God
13	God	8	God
16	God	9	God
2:23	God	8:14 (2)	God
24	God	16	God
29	God	17	God
3:2	God	27	God
3	God	33 (2)	God
4	God	9:26	God
5	God	10:2	God
6	God	11:22 (2)	God
7	God	33	God
11	God	13:1 (2)	God
19	God	4 (2)	God
23	God	6	God
25	God	15:8	God
26	God	32	God
29	God	16:27	God
30	God		
4:3	God		
6	God		
20 (2)	God		
5:1	God		

TABLE V (continued)

ROMANS *(continued)*

Source	NWT	Source	NWT
2	God		
5	God		
8	God		
10	God		
11	God		
15	God		
6:10	God		
11	God		
13 (2)	God		
17	God		
22	God		
23	God		
7:4	God		
22	God		
25	God		
8:3	God		
7	God		
8:19	God		
21	God		
28 (2)	God		
31	God		
34	God		
39	God		
9:5	God		
6	God		
8	God		
11	God		
14	God		
16	God		
20	God		
22	God		
10:1	God		
3 (2)	God		
9	God		
11:1	God		
2 (2)	God		
8	God		
21	God		
23	God		

TABLE V (continued)
ROMANS *(continued)*

Source	NWT	Source	NWT
29	God		
30	God		
32	God		
12:1 (2)	God		
2	God		
3	God		
13:2	God		
14:3	God		
6 (2)	God		
10	God		
11	God		
12	God		
17	God		
18	God		
20	God		
22	God		
15:5	God		
6	God		
7	God		
9	God		
13	God		
15	God		
16	God		
17	God		
30	God		
33	God		
16:20	God		
26	God		

I CORINTHIANS

Arthrous (71)		*Anarthrous* (34)	
1:2	God	1:1	God
4 (2)	God	3	God
9	God	18	God
20	God	24 (2)	God
21 (3)	God	30	God
25 (2)	God	2:5	God
27 (2)	God	7	God
28	God	3:9 (3)	God

TABLE V (continued)

I CORINTHIANS (continued)

Source	NWT	Source	NWT
29	God	16	God
2:1	God	23	God
7	God	4:1	God
9	God	6:9	God
10 (2)	God	10	God
11 (2)	God	19	God
12 (2)	God	7:7	God
14	God	19	God
3:6	God	24	God
7	God	40	God
10	God	8:4	God
16	God	5 (2)	gods
17 (3)	God	6	God
3:19	God	9:21	God
4:5	God	10:20	God
9	God	31	God
20	God	11:7	God
5:13	God	12:3	God
6:11	God	14:2	God
13	God	15:10	God
14	God	34	God
20	God	50	God
7:15	God		
17	God		
8:3	God		
8	God		
9:9	God		
10:5	God		
13	God		
32	God		
11:3	God		
12	God		
13	God		
16	God		
22	God		
12:6	God		
18	God		
24	God		
28	God		

TABLE V (continued)
I CORINTHIANS *(continued)*

Source	NWT	Source	NWT
14:18	God		
25 (2)	God		
28	God		
33	God		
36	God		
15:9	God		
10	God		
15 (2)	God		
24	God		
28	God		
38	God		
57	God		

II CORINTHIANS

Arthrous (51)		*Anarthrous* (28)	
1:1	God	1:1	God
3 (2)	God	2	God
4	God	12	God
9	God	20	God
12 godly sincerity		21	God
18	God	2:17 (2)	God
19	God	3:3	God
20	God	5:1	God
23	God	5	God
2:14	God	11	God
15	God	13	God
17	God	19	God
3:4	God	21	God
5	God	6:4	God
4:2 (2)	God	7	God
4 (2) the god, God		16 (3)	God
6 (2)	God	7:1	God
7	God	9 in a godly way	
15	God	10 in a godly way	
5:18	God	11 in a godly way	
20 (2)	God	8:5	God
6:1	God	11:2 a godly jealousy	
16	God	12:19	God
7:6	God	13:4 (2)	God

TABLE V (continued)
II CORINTHIANS (continued)

Source	NWT	Source	NWT
12	God		
8:1	God		
16	God		
9:7	God		
8	God		
11	God		
12	God		
13	God		
14	God		
15	God		
10:4	God		
5	God		
13	God		
11:7	God		
11	God		
31	God		
12:2	God		
3	God		
21	God		
13:7	God		
11	God		
13	God		

GALATIANS

	Arthrous (19)		Anarthrous (12)	
	1:4	God	1:1	God
G	10	God	3	God
A	13	God	2:19	God
L	15	God	3:26	God
A	20	God	4:7	God
T	24	God	8 (2)	gods
I	2:6	God	9 (2)	God
A	20	God	14	God
N	21	God	5:21	God
S	3:6	God	6:7	God
	8	God		
	11	God		
	17	God		
	18	God		

TABLE V (continued)

GALATIANS (continued)

Source	NWT	Source	NWT
20	God		
21	God		
4:4	God		
6	God		
6:16	God		
1:3	God	1:1	God

EPHESIANS

Arthrous (24)		Anarthrous (7)	
17	God	2	God
2:4	God	2:8	God
10	God	4:6	God
16	God	24	God
19	God	6:17	God
22	God	23	God
3:2	God		
7	God		
9	God		
10	God		
19	God		
4:13	God		
18	God		
30	God		
32	God		
5:1	God		
2	God		
5	God		
6	God		
20	God		
6:6	God		
11	God		
13	God		

PHILIPPIANS

Arthrous (14)		Anarthrous (10)	
1:3	God	1:2	God
8	God	11	God
14	God	28	God
2:9	God	2:6 (2)	God

TABLE V (continued)
PHILIPPIANS *(continued)*

Source	NWT	Source	NWT
27	God	11	God
3:14	God	13	God
15	God	15	God
19	god	3:3	God
4:6	God	9	God
4:7	God		
9	God		
18	God		
19	God		
20	God		

COLOSSIANS

Arthrous (18)		Anarthrous (2)	
1:3	God	1:1	God
6	God	2	God
10	God		
15	God		
25 (2)	God		
27	God		
2:2	God		
12	God		
19	God		
3:1	God		
3	God		
6	God		
12	God		
17	God		
4:3	God		
11	God		
12	God		

I THESSALONIANS

Arthrous (27)		Anarthrous (9)	
1:2	God	1:1	God
3	God	9	God
4	God	2:4	God
8	God	5	God
9	God	13	God
2:2 (2)	God	2:15	God

TABLE V (continued)

I THESSALONIANS *(continued)*

Source	NWT	Source	NWT
4	God	4:1	God
8	God	16	God
9	God	5:18	God
10	God		
12	God		
13 (2)	God		
14	God		
3:2	God		
9 (2)	God		
11	God		
13	God		
4:3	God		
5	God		
7	God		
8	God		
14	God		
5:9	God		
23	God		

II THESSALONIANS

Arthrous (12)		*Anarthrous* (6)	
1:3	God	1:1	God
4	God	2	God
5 (2)	God	6	God
11	God	8	God
12	God	2:4 (2)	god, a god
2:4	God		
11	God		
13 (2)	God		
16	God		
3:5	God		

I TIMOTHY

Arthrous (7)		*Anarthrous* (15)	
1:11	God	1:1	God
2:3	God	2	God
4:3	God	4	God
5:4	God	17	God
21	God	2:5 (2)	God

TABLE V (continued)
I TIMOTHY *(continued)*

Source	NWT	Source	NWT
6:1	God	3:5	God
13	God	15 (2)	God
		4:4	God
		5	God
		10	God
		5:5	God
		6:11	God
		17	God

II TIMOTHY

Arthrous (10)		Anarthrous (3)	
1:3	God	1:1	God
6	God	2	God
7	God	8	God
2:9	God		
14	God		
15	God		
19	God		
25	God		
3:17	God		
4:1	God		

TITUS

Arthrous (7)		Anarthrous (6)	
1:2	God	1:1 (2)	God
3	God	4	God
2:5	God	7	God
10	God	16	God
11	God	3:8	God
13	God		
3:4	God		

PHILEMON

Arthrous (1)		Anarthrous (1)	
4	God	3	God

TABLE V (continued)
HEBREWS

Arthrous (54)		Anarthrous (14)	
Source	NWT	Source	NWT
1:1	God	1:6	God
8	God	2:9	God
9 (2)	God	3:4	God
2:4	God	12	God
13	God	6:1	God
17	God	5	God
4:4	God	18	God
9	God	8:10	God
10	God	9:14	God
12	God	10:31	God
14	God	11:3	God
5:1	God	16	God
4	God	12:22	God
10	God	23	God
12	God		
6:3	God		
6	God		
7	God		
10	God		
13	God		
17	God		
7:1	God		
3	God		
19	God		
25	God		
9:14	God		
20	God		
24	God		
10:7	God		
12	God		
21	God		
10:29	God		
36	God		
11:4 (2)	God		
5 (2)	God		
6	God		
10	God		
16	God		

TABLE V (continued)
HEBREWS *(continued)*

Source	NWT	Source	NWT
19	God		
25	God		
40	God		
12:2	God		
7	God		
15	God		
28	God		
29	God		
13:4	God		
7	God		
15	God		
16	God		
20	God		

JAMES

Arthrous (11)		Anarthrous (5)	
1:5	God	1:1	God
13	God	13	God
27	God	20	God
2:5	God	2:23	God
19	God	3:9	God
23	God		
4:4 (2)	God		
6	God		
7	God		
8	God		

I PETER

Arthrous (19)		Anarthrous (19)	
1:3	God	1:2	God
2:12	God	5	God
15	God	21 (2)	God
17	God	23	God
3:4	God	2:4	God
17	God	5	God
18	God	10	God
20	God	16	God
4:11 (2)	God	19	God
14	God	20	God

TABLE V (continued)
I PETER *(continued)*

Source	NWT	Source	NWT
16	God	3:5	God
17	God	21	God
19	God	22	God
5:2	God	4:2	God
5	God	6	God
6	God	10	God
10	God	11	God
12	God	5:2	God

II PETER

Arthrous (5)		*Anarthrous* (2)	
1.1	God	1:17	God
2	God	21	God
2:4	God		
3:5	God		
12	God		

I JOHN

Arthrous (57)		*Anarthrous* (3)	
1:5	God	3:1	God
2:5	God	2	God
14	God	4:12	God
17	God		
3:8	God		
9 (2)	God		
10 (2)	God		
17	God		
20	God		
21	God		
4:1	God		
2 (2)	God		
3	God		
4	God		
6 (3)	God		
7 (3)	God		
8 (2)	God		
9 (2)	God		

TABLE V (continued)
I JOHN *(continued)*

Source	NWT	Source	NWT
10	God		
11	God		
15 (3)	God		
16 (4)	God		
20 (2)	God		
21	God		
5:1	God		
2 (2)	God		
3	God		
4	God		
5	God		
9 (2)	God		
10 (2)	God		
11	God		
12	God		
13	God		
18 (2)	God		
19	God		
20 (2)	God		

II JOHN

Arthrous (0)		*Anarthrous* (2)	
		3	God
		9	God

III JOHN

Arthrous (3)		*Anarthrous* (0)	
6	God		
11 (2)	God		

JUDE

Arthrous (1)		*Anarthrous* (3)	
4	God	1	God
		21	God
		25	God

TABLE V (continued)
REVELATION

Arthrous (93)		*Anarthrous* (2)	
Source	*NWT*	*Source*	*NWT*
1:1	God	7:2	God
2	God	21:7	God
6	God		
8	God		
9	God		
2:7	God		
18	God		
3:1	God		
2	God		
12 (4)	God		
14	God		
4:5	God		
8	God		
11	God		
5:6	God		
9	God		
10	God		
6:9	God		
7:3	God		
10	God		
11	God		
12	God		
15	God		
17	God		
8:2	God		
4	God		
9:4	God		
13	God		
10:7	God		
11:1	God		
11	God		
13	God		
16 (2)	God		
17	God		
19	God		
12:5	God		
6	God		
10 (2)	God		

TABLE V (continued)
REVELATION (continued)

Source	NWT	Source	NWT
17	God		
13:6	God		
14:4	God		
7	God		
10	God		
12	God		
19	God		
15:1	God		
2	God		
3 (2)	God		
7	God		
8	God		
16:1	God		
7	God		
9	God		
11	God		
14	God		
19	God		
21	God		
17:17 (2)	God		
18:5	God		
8	God		
20	God		
19:1	God		
4	God		
5	God		
6	God		
9	God		
10	God		
13	God		
15	God		
17	God		
20:4	God		
6	God		
21:2	God		
3 (2)	God		
10	God		
11	God		
22	God		

TABLE V (continued)

REVELATION *(continued)*

Source	*NWT*	Source	*NWT*
23	God		
22:1	God		
3	God		
5	God		
6	God		
9	God		
18	God		
19	God		

TABLE VI

THE OCCURRENCES OF ΣΩΤΗΡ IN THE PASTORALS

Explicitly of God		*Explicitly of Christ*		*Of Both*	
I Timothy	1:1				
	2:3				
	4:10	II Timothy	1:10		
Titus	1:3	Titus	1:4		
	2:10			Titus	2:13
	3:4		3:6		

SCRIPTURE INDEX

INDEX OF PERSONS AND TOPICS